Shower of Jewels

FENG SHUI:
An Amusing Yet
Practical Guide to
Ancient Principles
of Placement
and Geoenergy
Manipulation

Richard Teh-Fu Tan, O.M.D., L.Ac.
Cheryl Warnke, L.Ac.

SAN DIEGO, CALIFORNIA

Dedicated to our Fathers:

Yi-Pei Tan
Joseph Warnke

Mail inquiries to: Feng Shui
P.O. Box 420984, San Diego, CA 92142

Editors: Keith Robbins, Harvey Berger
Composition and illustration: Cheryl Warnke
Photography: Richard Tan, Denise DeLuise,
Sharon Cox, Cheryl Warnke
Calligraphy: Richard Tan

Printed in San Diego, 1996
First edition

ACKNOWLEDGMENTS

We would like to express our heartfelt thanks to the Tan family: Fangfang, Litton, Waylee, and Wiselee; Marilyn Hoffman for her inspiration during the inception of this project; and Harvey Berger for contributing his creative skills in writing and editing. Others we would like to thank who have made contributions are: James Allyn Moser, Jackie Bensinger, Keith Robbins, and our friends and patients for their love and support.

TABLE OF CONTENTS

To Our Readers

    If there was a way you could change destiny to work in your favor, wouldn't you be curious? Feng Shui (pronounced "fung schway"), the study and art of placement, has become increasingly popular in the West, and people are claiming fantastic results with it. Feng Shui can help us recognize the universal forces that influence our lives through our environment, and it can teach us how to alter these forces to our benefit.

    There is a natural curiosity about Feng Shui because everyone is seeking a formula for success. It is intriguing, and you could say it is a little mystifying. Most of all it's fun. So this book is intended to be an entertaining introduction. We tried to write it in a form you can easily understand and immediately apply to your own life. Become excited! Feng Shui can work miracles for you.

    Dr. Richard Tan, the inspiration for this book, has been practicing acupuncture in the United States and Taiwan for over twenty years. He became interested in Feng Shui many years ago, in an effort to even more effectively help his patients. He is known today not only as one of the most competent and renowned acupuncturists in North America, but as a master of Feng Shui.

Cheryl Warnke, an associate of Dr. Tan, has been one of his few personal students, and is a practitioner of his unique acupuncture style. Over the years, Cheryl has combined her interests in Chinese Medicine with Feng Shui, providing her patients with the best of holistic health, for their body and their environment.

True stories of Feng Shui readings performed by Dr. Tan determined the writing style we used and are the primary teaching tool, posing situations that are commonly encountered in everyday life. The summaries at the end of each story provide even more useful information and insights. We also chose simple illustrations and photos not only to complement the stories, but also show how Feng Shui is expressed in classical and modern architecture.

The basic fundamentals of Feng Shui are explained in the first five chapters. Don't worry though, there isn't any difficult mathematics or dry intellectual verbiage to get lost in—it's just simple, applicable Feng Shui. We also included a chapter of ancient mystical legends, full of great wisdom and wit. They alone could make you a believer!

We hope you enjoy reading about this time-tested, thought-provoking subject. Who knows, it may bring you good luck, love, and boundless prosperity! We believe you will find *Shower of Jewels* useful as well as enormously entertaining.

CHAPTER 1: WHAT IS FENG SHUI?

We are profoundly influenced by our environment, both consciously and subconscious, as we continuously interact with it on many levels. We are seemingly bombarded on a daily basis through various media about our air quality and the nutritional value of our food. We are influenced physically and psychologically by the natural environment, as well as our artificial manmade spaces: our offices, buildings, homes, and so on.

If you have ever walked into a friend's home and realized that you were positively influenced by the decor and ambience, you have had a Feng Shui experience. Maybe you didn't stop to consider the dynamics of what "made the space work," but you intuitively sensed nonetheless that the home was pleasing. Feng Shui is the art, the science, and the study of those dynamics. It is the recognition of what creates a positive energetic force, or a detrimental one—and the reaping of those benefits derived from being surrounded by good forces, as well as recognizing and changing undesirable ones.

At first glance, Feng Shui may seem a bit technical. On the other hand, it may seem a little mystical or superstitious. You wouldn't necessarily be wrong in either case. There are many elements in Feng Shui, but it can be quite simple to grasp. We want to present a basic understanding of Feng Shui principles, so in essence this book can be considered a primer. Yet with the insights gained as you read this book—"knowledge of the placement and nature of things"—you will learn basically everything you need to make corrections to your home or business. You will gain a sense of natural energy flow, and an insightful viewpoint about your surroundings—but, most importantly, a valuable sense of control over your environment. By using Feng Shui, you can feel less like a hapless victim of your surroundings and circumstances. You can gain the power to create an environment that will work to your advantage.

Employing the simple ideas you can gain from this book may well improve the quality of your life! Sleeplessness can be alleviated, relationships can be made smoother, and optimal emotional and physical health can be accentuated using Feng Shui. For example, after reading this book, you may discover that your bed is located in a position that is bad Feng Shui. You may rest better after moving it to a better location.

Much of Chinese culture has been assimilated into our Western way of life. Chinese martial arts, such as Kung Fu or Tai Qi, are widely practiced on every continent. There probably isn't a Westerner who hasn't at least tried Chinese food. And everybody in the West has heard of Chinese acupuncture. But what is Feng Shui? Most people have never heard of it, for as familiar and ancient as it is in the Orient, it has only been recently exposed to Westerners. So what exactly does the Chinese term Feng Shui mean? The written Chinese character Feng (風) means wind; Shui (水) means water. These two characters together, Feng Shui (or "Wind" and "Water") is the term used to describe the flow and accumulation of energy (or "Qi" in Chinese, pronounced "chee"). Feng Shui is a very appropriate term because we are most influenced by the Qi in our environment in the dynamic, constantly moving elements of wind and water. Floods, hurricanes, and tornadoes are gross examples of the power of wind and water in their extremes; yet, without these two elements, life would not be possible.

As you may have guessed, Feng Shui is much more than simply studying the effects of wind and water. It is the study of subtle influences of energy and objects, and how they might affect us. Although subtle, these forces nonetheless can, over a period of time, have a profound effect on your health, mental state, relationships, and even your finances.

Throughout the long history of China, Feng Shui has been gathered into a vast body of empirical knowledge. There have been numerous volumes written over a 2,000 plus year documented history on the subject of Feng Shui. Some of the ancient stories and texts are colorful and mystical, but these concepts have expanded and matured through time, so Feng Shui is regarded not only as an art form, but if you will, a set of maxims based on countless experiences—a body of universal truths.

Outside Chinese culture the concept of Feng Shui may initially seem strange, but it is really based on good common sense, sensitivity to the environment, and observations of psychological influences. You will be happy to know that Feng Shui is applicable to your personal situation, and you can immediately use what you have learned. It can teach you how to make the choices that are "energetically correct" when applied to architecture, landscaping, interior design, or simply arranging your living room furniture.

Hopefully, the view we present on Feng Shui will provide a glimpse into Eastern thought. It is artistic, colorful, and can broaden our Western analytical minds. You will see the world from a completely different viewpoint (through the eyes of Feng Shui), and will automatically notice the Feng Shui everywhere you go. For example, Cheryl, the co-author, instantly knew why a certain restaurant she dined at once with a friend was not busy, although the food and service were excellent. There was a huge planter placed directly in front of the door creating an energetic barrier. It made the restaurant feel uncomfortable to enter. A potential patron walking by, if he were at all hesitant, would be swayed from dining there by this "wall of Qi."

QI MEANS MORE THAN ENERGY

It would be literally impossible to explain what Feng Shui is about without describing the concept of "Qi." The closest translation of Qi into English is the word "energy." But Qi as described in Oriental terms is a vast concept entailing more

The character for Qi is of a
rice pot with rising steam.

description than an English dictionary can offer. Qi is a foundation basic to Chinese medicine, thought, philosophy, and martial arts. By understanding the concept of Qi, you can begin to understand Chinese language, culture, and subsequently, Feng Shui. You must understand Qi to use Feng Shui.

Many terms in the Chinese language are more "circular" (less analytical, but more conceptual) in comparison to English. Often, a term will have many meanings, according to the historical significance gained through time. But it will also have yet another meaning, sometimes requiring careful explanation as well as a story line! Qi is one of those "many meaning terms" in Chinese, but it is not too difficult to understand.

According to Chinese thought, Qi may be expressed as kinetic energy, but also can be described as potential energy. It also can be static matter capable of conversion to either kinetic or potential energy. Qi is formless as electricity or air, but can also be described as the essence derived from coarser substances, such as food or nature. Yet, it is not as complex as it seems: Simply, everything in the universe has inherent within it the invisible force of Qi—the primary force for existence is Qi.

The Chinese have a deep connection to Qi and how it affects every aspect of their lives. Actually, the term "Qi" is used in everyday conversation. If a person becomes easily angered and holds onto it for a long time, he may said to have too much "Huo Qi" (Fire Qi), meaning that he has angry Qi, making him touchy and intolerable. When describing a person's taste in clothing, a Chinese-speaking woman may turn to her friend and whisper that another has "Tu Qi" (Soiled Qi), meaning that the victim of their gossip has poor fashion taste. When a Chinese person pays respect to the deceased he may describe the eerie feelings he felt at the graveyard as "Han Qi" (Freezing Qi), describing a sad, cold, and lifeless place. If a woman feels exhausted after a long day, she will say she has lost her "Li Qi" (Strength Qi) meaning she doesn't have the strength to go on!

In Chinese Medicine the sensation at the acupuncture needle when inserted into the skin and twirled is called "Deh Qi" (Grasp It Qi), meaning the needle found the Qi within the body. Both co-authors are acupuncturists, and when the "Deh Qi" arrives as the needle is stimulated we are assured that the treatment will be effective, because the healing Qi has been activated in the patient's body.

In reference to Feng Shui, we want to understand the "Di Qi" (Qi of the entire Earth). Di Qi is the total expression of the earth's Qi from everything living and nonorganic, even including the atmosphere. We felt the closest translation of Di Qi from Chinese to English would be "Geoenergy." However, Qi cannot simply be considered energy; it includes unquantifiable qualities such as emotion, fashion, color, and intuition.

FENG SHUI
THE RIGHT WAY

Where do you start with Feng Shui? If you are reading this book in your living room, it might become the object of your first Feng Shui critique. The interior of the house is easier to notice somehow, but Feng Shui is also concerned with everything outside. For example, the walkway to the house, the lot, the neighborhood, the natural environment, and manmade things. Actually, Feng Shui outside the dwelling is the most important aspect to consider before going indoors. Proper Feng Shui requires a largest-picture perspective, then smaller details. Take care not to make the mistake of looking only at the interior Feng Shui, and neglecting your entire external environment.

It is also easy to become caught up in the idea of "gain great riches through Feng Shui!" Actually, the main purpose of Feng Shui is to avoid or reduce the negative Qi in our environment. Good things can happen with a healthful environment, but enhancing the Feng Shui is not the lazy man's way to make a fortune.

THE "MASTERS"

In many Chinese communities, it is common practice to have a Feng Shui consultation when considering the purchase of a home, or leasing a place of business. There are professional Feng Shui practitioners who for a fee will give a reading to a customer. Even though there are countless books available in Chinese, a Feng Shui master will often discover an error the customer was unaware of. Also, there are several aspects of Feng Shui to consider during a reading. It is easy to overlook otherwise obvious things when you are accustomed to a work or living space—even easier to miss important intricate details. A talented master will usually come up with brilliant, cost-effective, and easily implemented suggestions to correct the Qi.

But for all intents and purposes, what can be gained from this book will be sufficient for you to do your own readings, unless you are considering a sizable real estate purchase or implementing an expensive building plan. In this case, a thorough Feng Shui reading by a master may be worth the investment.

We would like to convey that Feng Shui has a place in our modern, scientific, industrialized world. We present it as a common-sense system to perceive our surroundings, and usually, it is something that you were already, somehow, intuitively aware of. It just needs to be clarified into a practical, usable form you can take advantage of.

After reviewing some of the basic principles—the skeletal make-up of Feng Shui—you will see how things "fit together," and how the Chinese sages "figured it all out." To understand the effect Qi has on yourself and those around you is an empowering tool. Use Feng Shui to make changes in your life, and you will become one with the flow of "Wind" and "Water."

CHAPTER 2:
ANCIENT
LEGENDS

Feng Shui

SHOWER OF JEWELS

The "Yin Style" Feng Shui master, Guo Pu, who lived during the Jin dynasty (276–324 A.D.) was credited with writing the "Book of Burying the Dead." It was a guide-line of instruction for the proper and most respectful way to bury ancestors. Legends say this book was written by him, but to this day there is still argument if he actually was the author because of lost information due to the passage of time—almost 1800 years.

The care and respect for the deceased called "Yin Style" Feng Shui was the foundation for modern "Yang Style" Feng Shui, care for the living. Actually, Yin Style Feng Shui was the only kind practiced. Yang Style did not exist until relatively recently.

In ancient China, much depended on the respect paid to your ancestors. And, in this story, perfect Feng Shui made the difference between prosperity and poverty.

ONCE UPON A TIME Guo Pu was discussing Feng Shui with Mr. Gin, one of his close friends, who was a high-ranking officer in the central government. Young Guo Pu was already widely respected for his knowledge of Feng Shui, but his friend was skeptical. During one of their animated conversations, Guo Pu stated: "Although a person may not have inherited riches and may be very poor, he can become wealthy if he cares for his deceased ancestors by choosing an honorable burial plot. If he follows this, his ancestors will bestow great blessings on him." Mr. Gin became obstinate: "You think you are such an expert in ancestral Feng Shui, but I am very skeptical that a poor man could become wealthy from such trivial contrivances!"

Both of them were stubborn and unyielding, so after debating long into the night, they made a bet. They came up with the idea of finding an honest hard-working man, comparatively poor to the rest of society, to be their test subject.

They journeyed to a simple village, and went to the poorest section. They found a man there with ragged clothes sitting in front of his door. He told the two men he was depressed because he was only a poor carpenter barely able to feed his little family. After Guo Po and Mr. Gin spoke to the man for a while they agreed that he was an ideal test subject. With the agreement of Mr. Gin, Guo Pu approached the carpenter and asked: "Would you like to be wealthy and make a great fortune? After hearing your story Mr. Gin would like to help you and your family." Mr. Gin stepped forward and held out a big bag of silver coins to the carpenter. "I hope you use this money for business, or invest it to generate more profit—that would make my friend and me very happy."

The carpenter accepted the bag of silver coins and was overjoyed by the blessing bestowed from these two men. It truly was jewels showered down from heaven. He jumped up and down and even pinched his own cheek to make sure that it was not just a dream. After several minutes of blind elation, he began to calm down. He turned to thank the two men, but they had quietly disappeared.

The carpenter didn't know what to do with so much money, so he took a few silver coins to buy groceries and small items that his family desperately needed. Then he carefully packed the rest of the money and tied it onto his belt. He rushed to the market to select a big piece of the best meat and a fresh fish to bring to his wife. He was overjoyed and danced on his way home.

Suddenly, a huge, hungry eagle swooped down and tried to snare the fish from the carpenter's hands. He tried to protect the fish by twisting his body and waving his hands to stop the bird. Unexpectedly, the eagle grabbed the money bag instead of the prospective dinner and flew far away. The carpenter was crushed, having only two meals to show for his lost fortune.

Three years passed before Guo Pu and Mr. Gin returned to the village to find the carpenter. They found him in the same poor condition sitting on his front step. The carpenter told Mr. Gin the sad story, and expressed his despair over his lost fortune. This disappointed Mr. Gin very much, but he decided to give the carpenter another bag of silver coins saying: "Be very careful, look after the money and use it in a clever way to generate more fortune."

The carpenter thanked him with tears, then carefully wrapped the money away layer by layer, and brought it home quickly and secretly. He hid it in the bottom of a very large vase for safekeeping, using only a few coins to buy material for his carpentry business. Unfortunately, he did not tell his wife the money was in the vase. When she came home and noticed that there was no more food left to feed the family, she decided to sell the vase to buy some rice. When the carpenter came home and learned what happened to the money, he nearly went insane with grief and despair.

The next year Guo Pu and Mr. Gin came back to visit the carpenter. This time he begged forgiveness for his careless misfortune. "You treated me so kindly by twice giving me money. I didn't even get a chance to enjoy it or use it for a greater purpose."

When Mr. Gin realized what happened, he decided to give him yet another bag of money: "This is your last chance; I hope that by next year when we come back you will be very successful."

This time the carpenter grabbed the bag of money so tightly he hurt his hand. He rushed home, but first showed his wife, so together they could find the safest place to hide it for safekeeping. They decided to wait until night and bury the money at the inside corner of their house. Because of this sneaky late night activity, a passing thief noticed and peeked through a crack in the front door. He saw everything that was going on, and later that night broke into the house when the couple was sound asleep. He dug the money out of the hole and scooped everything into his bag, including the dirt and ashes. He ran away, leaving the carpenter penniless once more.

Guo Pu and Mr. Gin returned for the third time, and the poor, depressed carpenter was still in ragged clothes. So Guo Pu turned to Mr. Gin and smugly said: "Now it is my turn, you tried three times and did not succeed; I will only allow myself one chance." Mr. Gin bowed honorably to Guo Pu and told him to please try his method.

Guo Pu received permission from the carpenter to journey to the grave site where his parents' bones were buried. Guo Pu personally chose another site to relocate the remains of the carpenter's ancestors. (Of course this grave site had very good Feng Shui, called "dragon cave": a cave where a lucky dragon could possibly live.) Guo Pu told him to have hope. From now on good fortune would be bestowed on his family. The carpenter and his wife thanked Guo Pu politely, but were doubtful in their hearts, having experienced so many previous disappointments. But they enjoyed their walk home, and on the way the carpenter noticed a piece of lead on the side of the road. He picked it up because he thought it might be useful someday. His wife laughed at him and said: "What good is that useless castoff?" A few days passed, and one evening, the neighbor's wife knocked at the carpenter's door. She was looking for lead to make weights for her husband, who was a fisherman. It was very scarce and she had been searching all over the village. Finally, the carpenter's house was her last hope.

Actually, before she arrived at the carpenter's house she promised God that if she could find lead for her husband, she would give that person the first catch from her husband's nets. She was surprised that her next-door neighbor had the precious lead and happily brought it home and told her husband.

Interestingly enough, the fisherman had a huge catch that first day out, and gave it to the carpenter as promised. The carpenter handed the fish to his wife, who decided they would eat only a few and cure the rest for later. While she was cleaning the fish, she found a ping pong ball-sized object inside the belly of one of them. It was shiny and translucent. She thought it would be a good toy marble for their little son. As he played with it, it glistened under the light of the harvest moon. One evening, as the little boy was playing on the street in front of his house with the luminous marble, a man passing by stopped to watch. The next day he approached the little boy and asked him to take him to his mother. He very much wanted to buy the pretty marble and was willing to pay a single silver coin for it. He smiled and said he wanted it as a little gift for his own child.

Actually, this man was a dishonest jeweler and knew the value of the marble, which as it turned out, was a priceless gemstone. The couple was unaware of its value, and agreed to sell it for a meager silver coin, which to them was a lot of money. However, the little boy refused to give it up at any price, so they did not sell it. The jeweler came again a few days later with two silver coins for the marble. The carpenter started becoming suspicious about the jeweler's persistence and wondered if the marble was indeed valuable. This time the carpenter taunted the jeweler and said: "How dare you offer a few measly coins, this is a precious stone and you insult us with this offer?" The jeweler thought he was found out and humbly asked: "What price are you asking?" The carpenter did not have any idea of its true value and held out both hands showing all ten fingers: "This is how much."

The jeweler thought that the carpenter wanted 10,000 silver coins. He scratched he head while he calculated, and finally decided. "Deal. I will pay you 10,000 coins for it." The carpenter never dreamed he could sell the marble for 10,000 pieces of silver. He had suddenly become very rich.

He wisely chose to invest the money to build stores and rent them out. He also hired people to operate his carpentry business. Because of his hard work and wise investments, money began to snow-ball into the carpenter's hands. Three years later, Guo Pu and Mr. Gin returned to visit the carpenter. He was no longer a poor man on his doorstep, but had become one of the wealthiest and most influential businessmen in the whole province. His name has been written in history as the famous and wise merchant, Mr. Liu.

Summary

At times in Chinese history ancestor worship verged on obsession: monopolizing the living with mysticism, superstition, and ritual. These practices are an inherent tradition of some schools of Feng Shui, and how you want to approach it depends on your individual taste.

The endurance and longevity of Chinese history have been interwoven and ingrained into everything Chinese. The mind set has been that of acceptance and openmindedness. This is because there is just too much information to either reject, accept, or fully understand. Keep this perspective as you study other styles of Feng Shui; there is more to learn than could be absorbed in a lifetime.

THE DRAGON EGGS

The main character in this legend, Fu Lin, followed the "rules and instructions" in Feng Shui, and he achieved the desired result. But he did not follow the spirit of Feng Shui: the tenets of honesty and good virtue. He lived in denial of his dishonest act, until he paid the ultimate price at his greatest moment of achievement.

A MAN NAMED CHEN escaped from the army during the Chinese civil war in the 1820s. He ran from the Northern province to the South, desperately trying to escape the horrors of war. After running for several days in the summer heat, he was near death from exhaustion and collapsed on a bridge that led into a small village. He fell into a deep sleep, tossed and turned because of a frightening dream, and fell off the bridge.

Meanwhile Mr. Lin, a tofu seller, was taking an afternoon nap at his little stand underneath the bridge. Mr. Lin was having a daydream the same time Chen was. In his dream, Mr. Lin saw a beautiful dragon staggering across the bridge overhead. The dragon fell off the bridge into the river below. Mr. Lin was startled and woke from his dream, fearing the dragon would fall on him. At the exact same moment, Chen fell off the bridge and into the river below. But he was unable to swim and shouted for help. Because Chen's falling off the bridge happened at the same time as the dragon falling in his dream, Mr. Lin decided this man must represent the dragon, so jumped into the river and saved him.

From then on, Mr. Lin believed this young man Chen was the beautiful dragon of luck in his dream, and decided to take him as his own child. He had only one daughter, and always desired to have a son. By taking him in, he also spared Chen from returning to the army. Mr. Lin loved his adopted son very much and decided Chen should marry his daughter so they could be related by law. However, Mr. Lin gave one condition to Chen: that the firstborn son must have the Lin family name. (This was not uncommon in Chinese culture, especially when an affluent family had no son to carry forth the family name.)

Chen respectfully named their firstborn son Fu Lin. Their son grew up, but unfortunately he did not inherit very much, except the tofu business. However, Fu Lin learned how to make very good tofu, and they had a very simple life. It is very hard work making tofu because you must get up very early to make soya bean juice, form the curd, and then go to the market every day. Tofu is a very popular Chinese food, even more than cheese is in the United States, so he was very busy.

One morning very early while it was still dark, Fu Lin was busy making tofu when he saw two lights from far away coming closer and closer. He was frightened because it was very dark and he imagined they were ghosts. But when he heard their voices, he was relieved because then he knew they were human. He was curious, so he quietly sneaked up on them to eavesdrop. He moved close enough to see them, and noticed that one man was dressed in Taoist priest robes, and the other man was dressed in the style of a Confucionist.

The two men were talking about the day they passed near Chen's little village and found a piece of land that had perfect Feng Shui. It was auspiciously shaped as a "dragon nest." What this means in Feng Shui is that it was nest-shaped, which is where good Qi could accumulate and bring great luck. They were checking this amazing place in the early morning so that nobody else would find out about it.

But the Confucionist challenged the Taoist priest. He was skeptical about Feng Shui, and said: "How can you prove this parcel of land has perfect Feng Shui?" The Taoist knew the Confucionist would challenge him, and before he finished speaking, the Taoist pulled two eggs from his pocket. He buried them in the center of the dragon's nest with his bare hands. After he finished, he brushed off his hands and clothes, and said that tomorrow they would return. The Taoist predicted the eggs would hatch in only one day because of the powerful Qi of this place, and the chicks would be running around when they returned.

Fu Lin watched this entire event, but to a tofu maker a dragons' nest is a scholar's dream, and the tofu business is very real. He had much work to do and was behind. After the two men left, Fu Lin had to work quickly to prepare the tofu to sell that day. No one else knew about the event, except the two men and Fu Lin.

Later that day, Fu Lin was busy selling tofu and all but forgot the early morning's strange occurrence. But after he finished work for the day, he recalled the event and decided to walk to the dragons' nest to see if the Taoist's words came true. When he found the place where the eggs were buried, he was surprised to see the beaks of two baby chicks trying to push their way out of the earth. He pulled them out of the dirt and they immediately began running around. He knew the Taoist's words were true about this spot being a lucky dragons' nest.

He thought if the Lin family could build a house in this spot they would become very wealthy and powerful. Fu Lin noticed the sun was beginning to set and realized the two men would be returning to see what happened to the eggs.

Fu Lin thought of an underhanded scheme to deceive these two men, and stop them from buying this land themselves. He ran quickly to his kitchen and grabbed two eggs, returned to the same spot, and buried them where the other two eggs were. He took the two baby chicks, ran far over the hill and released them. He wanted to be sure no one would discover what he had done.

At it approached midnight, two lantern lights appeared from far away and began moving closer and closer. The Taoist saw that the chicks did not hatch from the eggs and was very embarrassed. He sighed and said: "Maybe the perfect timing was off." They were so disappointed they turned their backs and left, never to return.

Fu Lin thought that he was very clever and was over-joyed as he watched them leave. The next few years he saved enough money to purchase the parcel of land and built a house on it. He moved his family to this dragons' nest place, and was anxious to have great luck, wealth, and power come to them.

Five years passed, and his son became one of the top ranking officers in the entire nation. The son brought them much power and wealth, and they did not have to do the tofu business anymore. Fu Lin was very proud because he had the best parcel of land in the entire province for his residence. His dreams seemed to be coming true.

Three more years passed, and Fu Lin's son became the highest ranking officer in the entire nation, and the right hand to the emperor. The family chose a proper day according to the I-Ching for the celebration of this wonderful appointment. The celebration was grand, only the emperor would have better. Fu Lin and his son had the honored positions at the head table, and there was much merriment, food, and wine. There were many delicacies presented: rare fishes, duck, squab, snake, and everything was specially prepared.

During the elaborate banquet, Mr. Lin was overjoyed because of his great luck and ate and drank freely, accepting each praise from his guests with a toast. His head was swimming with fine wine, when he noticed a beautiful egg dish that he was quite fond of. He had not eaten this dish for many, many years—funny, at that moment he couldn't remember the reason he had avoided it. He motioned the server to bring the eggs over to him, and Fu Lin greedily began to eat the dish. Suddenly, he started to choke after trying to swallow one of the eggs whole. No one could help him despite his silent, desperate beckoning, and he tragically choked to death among his honored guests.

Why were eggs the vehicle for Fu Lin's demise? Could it have been karma from the past because he used eggs in a dishonest scheme to gain the dragons' nest?

SECRET IN THE CERAMIC PILLOW

This famous legend from the Song Dynasty is about the famous I-Ching master, Shao Kang Jieh. It has been told for generations to students of the I-Ching, which is an integral part of Chinese culture, and the very foundation of Chinese astrology and Feng Shui.

Based on the Chinese horoscope, it can be determined which compass direction is most beneficial for you, which rooms or locations in the house are more favorable for you, and so on. We did not include Chinese astrology in this book; it merits treatment of its own on another occasion.

WHEN MR. CHAO was about 40 years old, he became obsessed with trying to unravel the many cryptic things that were spoken through the I-Ching. He was fervently studying one afternoon trying to understand its secrets.

He was so exhausted from his long hours of study that he decided to take a nap, but was disturbed by a rat running around in his room. He angrily threw his ceramic pillow at the rat, trying to hit it or at least scare it away. (In those times in China, pillows were made of ceramic and wrapped with cloth to make them comfortable.) The pillow struck the rat, but it got away unharmed. The pillow took the worst of it however, because it shattered when it hit the ground. Mr. Shao began to clean up the mess and noticed a little piece of paper that had fallen out of the pillow. Naturally, he picked it up, unfolded it, and read what was printed on it: "This pillow will be used to hit a rat and will break on XX day of XXX year." The date on the paper was today!

Mr. Shao was astounded by this incredible prediction. He knew that the author of the little note must be a great master of the I-Ching, and would beg him to become his teacher. Mr. Shao rushed to the shop where he bought the pillow to find out who made it. The shop owner told him it was made by a man who lived over a bridge on the other side of the village. He thanked the shop owner and ran out the door.

He arrived at the house completely out of breath. A man answered the door, but Mr. Shao was disappointed when the man explained that he was not the I-Ching master he had been searching for. The kindly man told him that the master had passed away. Mr. Shao was beside himself with desperation. Refusing to believe his own ears, he again pleaded to meet the author of the little note. Patiently, the man replied that the master had indeed passed away. However, before his death, he predicted that on this exact day a stranger would come looking for him, and become a famous student of his teachings. The man welcomed Mr. Shao inside and gave him the master's books. Shao Kang Jieh then went on to become one of the most famous I-Ching masters and founder of the "Plum Flower" style of I-Ching astrology. Books authored by him are the foundation of modern I-Ching astrology.

ROBE OF COMPASSION

Many people believe in the law of karma, or the principle that what goes around comes around. It is the same principle with Feng Shui. Han Lee lost his heart of integrity, humility, and compassion when he exploited Feng Shui for mere selfish means.

There is a saying that whenever we are privy to powerful information we become responsible for that gift and should respect and honor it. Traditionally, Feng Shui was passed verbally from the teacher. The student was expected to honor his teacher and the wisdom, and to develop a solid moral character.

IN A NORTHEAST PROVINCE in China lived a poor farmer named Han Lee. He worked very hard every day of his life struggling to support his family. One year near the time of Chinese New Year, he took his wife and children into a nearby village to buy gifts and a small amount of special food for the celebration. The journey was short, and they walked by a heavily wooded forest on the way.

The youngest child kept pulling the mother's shirt tail and pointing into the woods at something he saw. At first, the mother did not pay attention to him because they were in a hurry to go shopping, and she was daydreaming about the nice things she wanted to buy. But the child was persistent and began to cry, so Han Lee forged his way into the deep woods in the direction where the child was pointing.

Just a short distance away he discovered a Taoist man curled up behind a tree, huddling against the cold Mongolian wind. He was wearing thin clothes that were torn and dirty, and he shivered uncontrollably. Han Lee was surprised to find the man in such a state and knew he must take care of him, otherwise he would die within the hour. So Han Lee took off his robe and covered the Taoist with it. He returned to his family and told them they must postpone their journey to the village and carry the unfortunate stranger back to their home.

Han Lee's wife fed the Taoist hot soup and rice as he warmed himself near their tiny fire. After a while, the stranger felt life and strength returning to his limbs and began to talk as he ate. They became more acquainted as the evening wore on, and as it turned out the Taoist was a famous Feng Shui Master. As he was passing through the woods on his way to do a reading for a man near Han Lee's village, a band of thieves jumped out from the bushes and robbed him, taking his money, belongings, and even his warm robe. The Taoist began to cry because of his family waiting in anguish for him on this New Year's Eve. Han Lee's heart was moved, and he generously gave him the money they had saved for their own New Year's celebration and told him to return to his family. He even let the Taoist wear his only robe for the journey.

Fifteen days passed, and the Taoist found out that the kind man Han Lee, who saved his life and gave him money, was actually very poor. He wanted to show his gratitude, and decided to travel across the province in search of a piece of land that had perfect Feng Shui to present to Han Lee. Then Han Lee could move his ancestors' remains to that place and receive great blessings. Finally, the Taoist found an ideal parcel of land and brought Han Lee there, saying: "This is a perfect place to bury your ancestors' bones. If you do this, you and your children will inherit great blessings."

The Taoist used the I-Ching to choose a perfect day to move the graves of Han Lee's ancestors from the old gravesite to the new parcel. Years later, wonderful things began to happen for Han Lee's family. Not only did they have a bountiful harvest, but each year the harvest was larger and richer. The livestock produced healthy, strong offspring and his herds grew. Even though Han Lee was unable to read or write, he became a very successful farmer, and even started doing big business with crops and livestock.

Two decades passed, and Han Lee became the wealthiest man in the county. Unfortunately, he forgot his humble beginnings and had become greedy over the years. He was unsatisfied with his present good fortune and status and wanted even more. He knew that having the perfect burial ground for his ancestors had made a significant difference with his fortune, so he searched for another Feng Shui master to somehow make improvements or find an even better parcel so he could gain more riches. He hired a famous Feng Shui master and set out a very fancy dinner with expensive wine. They feasted and drank until late into the night. The next morning Han Lee woke early and could not wait another minute for the Feng Shui master, who was suffering from a wretched hangover. He yelled and shook him, finally pulling him out of bed to search for the perfect location for his ancestors' bones.

The Feng Shui master was in extremely bad humor, not even having hot tea to ease his pain. He begrudgingly climbed the hills and valleys and forded the creeks. He was unhappy because he had a very bad headache, but Han Lee pressed the master, asking him question after question. Han Lee became impatient because he thought the Feng Shui master was incompetent, and finally led him to the site the Taoist originally chose many years ago. Han Lee asked his opinion about the site where his ancestors were buried.

The Feng Shui master was panting heavily, and his head was spinning. By this time he just wanted to get rid of Han Lee, and go home to nurse his sick head. He waved his hand around and said the place was not good, and gave lame excuses to satisfy Han Lee's persistence. Han Lee kept asking for explanations, becoming increasingly agitated and demanding. The master racked his brains for any excuse and invented something to shut Han Lee up. He noticed the nearby creek and said that it symbolized Han Lee's money being swept away by the water. He said it was flowing in the wrong direction, and would adversely affect Han Lee's wealth. It was not the truth, of course, but he was sick of Han Lee's greedy persistence.

Han Lee asked how to improve the Feng Shui. The master said to have a new ditch dug to change the direction of the water flow. Lee was very greedy and decided to have it done as soon as possible, and hired ten men to work at the site. They worked hard day and night to change the creek, but even before they finished, water flooded everywhere. What they had done was to destroy the natural flow (the "dragon mouth"), and the whole place became a muddy swamp. It was no longer a pleasant little valley with a bubbling creek. At this time Han Lee tried to seek advice from the Feng Shui master, but he had fled to another province, knowing the advice he had given was wrong.

Han Lee's ancestors must have been unhappy with him because his luck began to change for the worse. The very next year his crops failed and then a three-year drought destroyed his farm. His livestock fell ill and died, reducing his once-massive herds to nothing. His wife became very cranky and mercilessly henpecked Han Lee day and night, and his children fled to more promising lands. He quickly grew poorer and poorer, reduced to a truly wretched state. Lee lost everything, but along the way he lost the most valuable thing of all: a heart of compassion and good will.

"Flying roof" architecture has been popular in Shanghai for centuries. In Feng Shui superstitions the roofs were said to protect against menacing flying devils—they would be impaled on the pointed corners if they flew too close! It was no coincidence that the shape was also appropriate for weather in Southern China, effectively shedding rainfall while providing maximum solar exposure.

CHAPTER 3:
THREE ELEMENTS OF PERFECTION

"The Golden Moment"

The purpose of Feng Shui is to bring you success. If you pick up this book and abide by every rule of Feng Shui for your place of business and your home, would you expect to automatically receive the benefits that were promised? It seems almost too easy. If it were that simple to achieve an unconditional guarantee, Feng Shui would gain incredible popularity in the West and would soon be considered a panacea for all mankind! Unfortunately, there is no absolute guarantee for success, but Feng Shui is one very important factor that can make the odds work in your favor. There are other key elements that cannot be ignored in creating the perfect environment, which is the foundation for true progress and prosperity. In other words, practicing Feng Shui exclusively is incomplete in the larger perspective of a person's life; the other pieces of the puzzle need to fit to make the complete picture.

In Chinese culture, people believe that in order to have success three important elements should be present. The direct translations of these from Chinese are:

Heavenly Timing
Beneficial Location or Space
Harmonizing People

Simply put, in order to have a powerful, genuine, and positive outcome, we must have the perfect timing, perfect space, and perfect people. These are called the three elements of perfection because all three must be present for a perfect condition to exist. The study of Feng Shui will give us the idea or knowledge to choose the perfect space or location, or to improve on that space. But ultimately, having perfect Feng Shui does not guarantee us success, because there are two other important factors that should be present at the same time: the timing should be right; and the people who work with you, live with you, or somehow otherwise influence you, should be positive and uplifting.

There are, of course, times in our lives when all three elements are in place and things work out right for us—in these "golden moments" our luck and prosperity seem almost effortless. Following the three elements of perfection is a simple way for you to examine your life; then you can create the perfect condition—a near guarantee for success.

When you pick up this book you will read a lot of "happy-ending" cases. After improving their Feng Shui, the character in the story will begin to have more business, better relationships, more peace of mind, improved health, and so on. We believe that when these measures of success occurred, they already had in place the elements of timing and people; the Feng Shui adjustment just helped fulfill the element of correct space to create the perfect condition.

For instance, if you bought a fantastic home, and hired the best Feng Shui grand master to do your landscaping and interior design, but the people you lived with were not getting along with you, or had negative energy working against you, you will still have a miserable life! Or even if you have wonderfully skilled and moralistic people surrounding and working with you, and generating positive energy toward you, if the timing is not right, you may miss that moment when opportunity knocks. The realistic attitude towards Feng Shui is to consider it as only one aspect that can bring you success—and then to focus equal attention on selecting the correct timing, and finding people who have a positive influence on you. Of course, this includes improving your existing relationships if you find they are unhealthy or detrimental.

Correcting the Feng Shui may help you make the adjustment to determining the correct timing, and surrounding yourself with beneficial people. In other words, Feng Shui can guide you to make changes in the other two elements. To enhance the space which influences us is the easiest of the three elements to control. From our point of view the

43

hardest element to control is the timing. However, selecting more positive people to surround ourselves with, and releasing negative people that are intertwined in our lives, can be emotionally difficult. It may be morally improper and emotionally impossible to estrange ourselves from family or friends. Yet, we may be able to either improve our relationships, or make it such that negative people do not have such a great influence over us.

In Western societies, people generally improve their living or working spaces with whatever the current interior design schemes are. As of yet, there hasn't been a set of universal design guidelines until Feng Shui was introduced; it is still unheard of compared with Chinese Medicine or Chinese cuisine. In the West, much more emphasis is placed on determining the correct timing in some form or another, and on selecting compatible people to surround us. On the whole, making our lives fulfilling and happy is often a "shot in the dark." However, human nature is such that we intuitively seek the three elements of perfection. We try to determine the perfect timing by consulting with fortune tellers, psychics, or astrologers—or on a more practical level, by following the stock market, real estate market, or general trends.

We also try to surround ourselves with the most beneficial people—we "search for Mr. or Ms. Right," and we "work on our relationships." We study psychology, sociology, and consult counselors, friends, and self-help books to understand ourselves and others.

However, as you probably figured out by now, finding the perfect people doesn't just mean looking for perfection in others. The most important person to focus on for achieving the "perfect person" is oneself. We must cultivate our own standards for virtue, morality, and integrity so we attract those with those same qualities (perfect people). We must pursue knowledge, wisdom, and good health so we can make educated decisions (perfect people, place, and timing). We also must develop patience and self-motivation, along with realistic goals (perfect timing).

There are many methods that man has developed to help determine perfect timing and choose compatible people. There are the more esoteric arts of face-reading, psychomancy, numerology, and astrology; as well as modern methods of psychologically based tests, statistics, price indexing, and geographical surveys. The Chinese I-Ching, which is thousands of years old, has long been a reference for determining the three elements of perfection (see Chapter 6 for explanation of I-Ching). Feng Shui masters often use the I-Ching in conjunction with a person's birthday in order to determine the ideal timing, matched with perfect surroundings, and appropriate people. In other words, the I-Ching is a vehicle to attain the three elements of perfection—used properly, it can be a very powerful tool.

In essence, what we want to convey is that Feng Shui can improve your space, but it is not infallible. If you correct something with Feng Shui, you might not get the quick result or the grand-finale fireworks you expected. All three elements of perfection must be fulfilled. Then you will experience one of those "golden moments" where everything will work out for you almost automatically and magically.

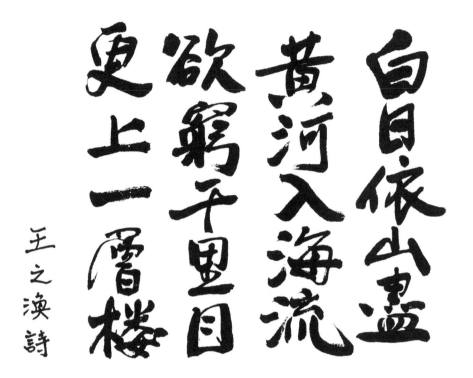

白日依山盡
黃河入海流
欲窮千里目
更上一層樓

王之渙詩

The sun is setting behind the towering hills.
The Yellow River is running into the vast ocean.
If you desire to see the most beautiful
view you must climb to the highest place.

CHAPTER 4:
SIX LEVELS
OF EXISTENCE
INFLUENCING
HUMANITY

質能象
數机感

We believe that ideal Feng Shui is based upon an understanding of what is most accurately translated from the Chinese as the "six levels of existence." Referencing the holistic concepts of "six levels of existence," which is a small part of the ancient I-Ching wisdom, will allow the Feng Shui practitioner to make beneficial decisions. The "six levels" are also a logical and invaluable guide to creative insights and solutions to alter reality—alter Feng Shui.

Utilizing any body of knowledge by ignoring the largest and most important issues first, and focusing on minute details out of context, will disempower that knowledge. That is why understanding these concepts of existence from

Chinese thought not only can greatly enhance one's understanding of Feng Shui, but also offers a holistic perspective of how the world works. Most appropriately translated from Chinese, these six levels are: substance or matter, energy, image, mathematics, chance, and feeling. We have also included another quality: that of intuition, which we believe is a unique human trait largely disregarded in modern Chinese thought.

SUBSTANCE OR MATTER

The most obvious level that affects us is the substance or material level. In Feng Shui the material level is, of course, the ultimate tool to instigate change. This level doesn't need explaining, but the other five dynamically interrelated levels directly influence matter. The six levels illustration (see page 54) is an oversimplification from a scientific viewpoint, but the real secret is to use energy, image, mathematics, chance, feeling, or intuition in a dynamic and creative way for Feng Shui manifestations to occur on the material level.

ENERGY

Energy coexists and is interdependent with matter. We need substance to convert into energy and we need energy for the existence of substance. For example, acupuncture needles (matter) are used to positively influence the energy (Qi) of the body so that it may function better. Matter and energy have an interchangeable and interdependent relationship that has no definitive beginning or end. One becomes and creates the other. The fundamental premise for the Feng Shui practitioner is to consider the effect of Qi on matter and vice versa, using either one to enhance or diminish the other.

IMAGE

The third level, image, means the picture, the shape, or style of something; in other words, its unique expression. Image is extremely meaningful to humankind—it defines and differentiates all matter. Water has particular qualities based on the physical joining of two hydrogen molecules at 109° angles to one oxygen molecule. The atoms (substance) and magnetic bond (energy) create a particular image. Image is the expression of all being, and Feng Shui practitioners use the power of image almost exclusively to make change on both the material and energetic levels. Feng Shui actually depends on the creative use of the interrelationship between image, matter, and energy. We often say in lectures that "In Feng Shui, image is everything."

The quality of a being is projected through its attributes: its appearance, weight, smell, and texture. For a simple example, why does an orange not look like a banana? Not only does the banana have the molecules that a banana has, but it also has a image specific to that of a banana. There is inherent within it the mystery of why a banana is what it is. But if a child sees a bowl of plastic fruit, his mind desires a banana from the image he sees. If a banana is his favorite fruit, a plastic banana would create a similar response in him as a real banana would (known in psychology as the

Pavlovian response). Image has a very powerful influence on the human mind. In terms of Feng Shui and altering Qi, it can be described as a kind of vibrational quality that affects all existence.

Image endows a specific vibration to matter and energy. The Egyptian pyramids are believed by many to have unexplainable power, quite possibly derived from the shape and peculiarities of these triangular-shaped monoliths. Feng Shui can create a desired image, which can then influence the environment. The style of dress one wears obviously projects a desired image—every good businessman knows the "dress for success" motto. The manner in which your house is decorated portrays a particular image, and that effect will create a specific energy—a desired feeling. This is what Feng Shui is all about. That is why placing a goldfish aquarium in the Southeast Ba Gwa corner (not compass direction) of your house may bring abundance or wealth—water meaning abundance, and the gold-colored fish meaning money, can create the image to obtain the desired result. When you place a plant in a certain area you are using living energy—the image of growth and life—and it will bring that positive energy into your life.

Math or Measurement

Math is defined as the science of number, quantity, and space. Mathematics gives humankind a concrete definition for the other six levels of existence. Science is based on the principles of mathematics and measurement, and the relationship between substance and energy is mathematically defined as $E = mc^2$. Mathematics provides us with incredible power—we can develop new chemical compositions, harness matter and energy, and even change their natural properties.

Many things we do involve math or measurement—from cutting the right length of board for a building project, to deciding the correct size painting to hang above the sofa. Mathematics and measurement are used quite extensively in Feng Shui. For example, a window may be too big in relation to the door or other objects—measurement is used to evaluate and to make correction. The Chinese I-Ching, which is used extensively in Feng Shui, is primarily based on logical mathematical permutations. Some schools of Feng Shui employ intricate calculations from a special compass called the loupan, deriving the exact degrees of measurement of buildings in relation to other structures.

CHANCE OR PROBABILITY

The fifth level, chance, is difficult for mankind to control. Many academic dissertations have been written involving "probability." It is an almost exhaustible subject because of the many possible outcomes. Probability is merely a ratio expressing the chances that a certain event will occur. Nothing is certain, and realistically the ratio means little in relation to the actual outcome. A meteorologist may forecast an 80 percent chance of rain for tomorrow, but then it doesn't rain. This happens often—nothing really is guaranteed. Mathematics and chance are related because mathematics is used to determine the odds, but chance is often based on risk-taking or trusting to luck against the odds.

But chance also makes our life exciting and interesting. What are the chances of finding the love of your life? What chance do you have of hitting the super lottery jackpot tonight? If we knew the exact answer to these questions using mathematics, then everyone would pick the same lottery numbers, and all hit the jackpot. Then, all would receive exactly one dollar for each dollar placed. It wouldn't be fun anymore because there aren't any chances. Using Feng Shui can improve our chances for success by making the odds work in our favor. Nothing is for sure, but wouldn't it be worth taking a chance on it?

FEELING

The sixth level is feeling, and the other five elements that influence humankind are incomplete without it. When you go to a place and spend time absorbing the atmosphere, you acquire a feeling from it. Let's say you want to correct the Feng Shui for the hallway in your home; you would logically select a traditionally used tool. But because of your feelings, you may choose to place something there which has special meaning to you. It turns out to be a much more effective cure—the difference being the feeling you used to make that choice.

Creating a positive emotion or feeling is the desired result of using Feng Shui. Humans are cognizant beings, emotion and feeling being primary attributes of our personalities. We want to feel good, and we sometimes base decisions on feeling, often disregarding logic (math or measurement), and going against all odds (chance). Feeling can be loosely defined as the result derived from the total effect of the environment: the marriage of substance, energy, image, mathematics, and chance. Feelings are relative to the individual's experience. However, humans share common universal feelings. This is why two people with entirely different personalities will most likely agree whether a Feng Shui environment is harmonious or not.

INTUITION

When we wrote this chapter we decided that intuition deserved a place of its own, separate from feeling, as the seventh level. Intuition is the finer expression of feeling—it is not just derived from feeling alone. It is the power of knowing or understanding something without reason; it goes beyond the other levels of existence. Psychic phenomena and other paranormal occurrences are examples of intuitive power.

Intuition is derived from the interconnectedness of all things, and this enhanced awareness—directed power of the mind—allows humans to have a special relationship with all beings. We can intuit that a friend may need our help. We may know something ominous occurred to a loved one, at the same moment in time, without any prior knowledge of the event. Or we may intuit that something unfortunate may happen to us if we follow an intended plan. There are many cases when travelers changed plans because they "felt" something was wrong, later to discover their intended flight ended in disaster. There are many times we think of

Six Levels of Existence
That Influence Humanity
Physically, Mentally, and Spiritually

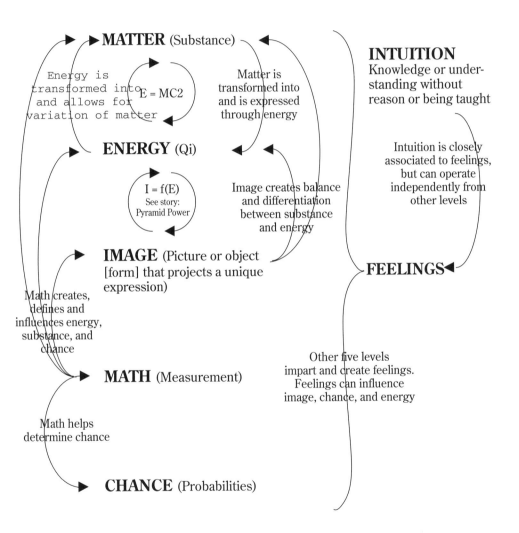

MATTER (Substance)

Energy is transformed into and allows for variation of matter

$E = MC2$

Matter is transformed into and is expressed through energy

ENERGY (Qi)

$I = f(E)$
See story:
Pyramid Power

Image creates balance and differentiation between substance and energy

IMAGE (Picture or object [form] that projects a unique expression)

Math creates, defines and influences energy, substance, and chance

MATH (Measurement)

Math helps determine chance

CHANCE (Probabilities)

INTUITION
Knowledge or under-standing without reason or being taught

Intuition is closely associated to feelings, but can operate independently from other levels

FEELINGS

Other five levels impart and create feelings. Feelings can influence image, chance, and energy

One or more of the levels can be creatively used to influence another. A scientific explanation is much more complicated than this simple diagram illustrates, but it has been simplified for use in Feng Shui.

someone we haven't thought about in a long time, and they call us the next day. Or, we get a nagging urge to call a relative, only to discover when we do that they were in some kind of trouble and needed our help.

Intuition often, but not always, of a higher order than feeling—it is not derived only from our surroundings, but from the spirit. Every being in the universe is connected to a shared consciousness; intuition is the cognizant connection with that force.

Intuition alone may not suffice to be the ultimate guide for decision making. Emotions are subjective and are not totally reliable, and intuition can be misguided. That is why it is important to consider the objective logic of other levels. Intuition, however, can confirm our choices in life, and in Feng Shui. Ultimately, through proper cultivation, intuition can become a connecting force for all of the six levels.

Intuition is a powerful human quality often unacknowledged in our logical, scientific, modern world. It can be the connection to all we hold as divine. Intuition can guide us to enhance our souls, and to create our sacred spaces.

Great wisdom, which transcends Feng Shui, can be gained by using the seven levels of existence in everything that is important to us.

Pyramid Power

Connecting the Six Levels of Existence with Measurement

T HE GREAT PYRAMID of Cheops, which is over 4,000 years old, is the last remaining of the Seven Wonders of the World. It is not known exactly why it was built, when, or what ancient people designed and constructed it. It remains a mystery to this day. Throughout history many have claimed there is great power associated with it, be it metaphysical, or derived from its incredible mathematically precise construction. There are those who swear there is a "pyramid power" that can be achieved when this famous Pyramid's dimensions are re-created.

This amazing Pyramid was designed using precise astronomical calculations; its foundation is perfectly oriented to true north. Even more fantastic is that the mathematical solutions required for its location and structure of angles and slopes display an advanced understanding of trigonometry! The structure incorporates a value for π, amazingly accurate to several decimal points, and π was quite intentionally expressed in several situations. Incorporated within the main chamber of the Pyramid is the famous Pythagoras triangle ratio [sum of the square of the two sides of a right triangle is equal to the square of the hypotenuse (long side of the triangle) or $(a^2 + b^2 = c^2)$]. Plato claimed these triangular dimensions were the foundation for existence of the cosmos in his book *Timaeus*.

It has been discovered that the Great Pyramid is a very precise almanac which measures the length of a year, including the .2422 fraction of a day that modern calendars clumsily account for as a leap year. Its alignment to due north is so perfectly accurate that it is a compass by which modern compasses are calibrated.

The great unknown architects of the Great Pyramid of Cheops knew the precise circumference of the planet, the length of the year to several decimals, and may well have known the length of the earth's orbit around the sun, the specific density of the planet, the acceleration of gravity, and even the speed of light.

The ancient Egyptians named their prime deity Hunab-Ku, sole dispenser of movement and measurement. The pyramid builders truly understood that it is measurement that defines and gives form to our physical reality. There is tremendous power and mystery still veiled within the Great Pyramid—and its perfect form can guide us to focus on the value and mysterious power of mathematics and measure.

What a profound find it would be if there were a computation to measure the effect of mathematics on image, feelings, or intuition! The relationship between energy and matter has been determined, but could the relationship between image (or idea) and matter be determined? We would like to put forth the hypothesis that not only does $E = mc^2$, but that Image=f(E). The E = Energy, the mathematical parameter, and f = effect upon. If one could compute this equation to determine the Image produced by Energy, then a scientific foundation could be established that would prove the effect of Feng Shui. You could find "Image" (for example the placement of a crystal in your wealth corner), and determine your results: "Energy" (your personal finances).

If a mastermind could figure out such an equation, it would open up possibilities to link physical reality with metaphysics and thought. It would link the specific "Image" qualities of form, design, and color—as well as the nonspecific "Image" qualities of will, intention, and imagination. Science has already crossed those boundaries to a degree with quantum mechanics; it is only a matter of time until the "Image Equation" is figured out. Could we measure and harness "pyramid power"? Could it be possible to measure and harness "Feng Shui power"? We hold many possibilities and much power in our hands; all that needs to be done is simple math.

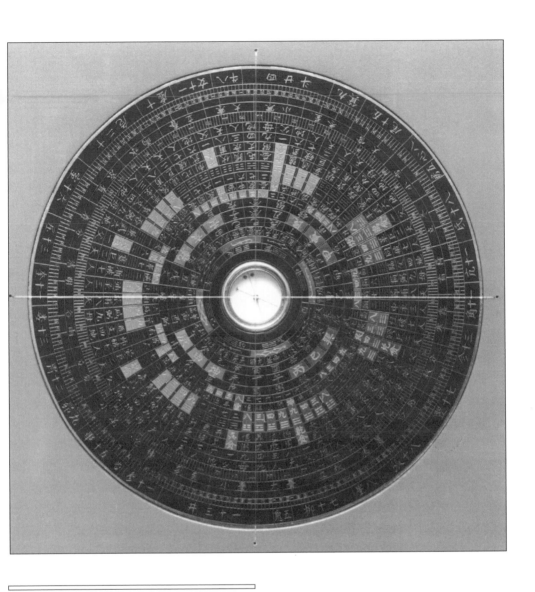

The loupan is a very complicated instrument used by the compass (Fukien) school of Feng Shui. It is magnetized with lodestone, and it is believed to have a sympathetic connection with the earth: it is used to determine the flow of the "Di Qi" (Qi of the earth). Consequently, it has always been regarded as an instrument of land, not sea. It is different from our concept of a compass in that the Chinese loupan is south pointing. It is also divided much differently than the Western compass. The loupan is composed of concentric circles, the number of rings varying, according to the complexity of the instrument. The rings correspond not only to Feng Shui, but also to Chinese astrology, astronomy, and philosophy.

CHAPTER 5: ROOTS AND BRANCHES

理氣 丘 巒頭

FENG SHUI ROOTS

The roots of Feng Shui can be found in ancient China approximately 500 B.C. In those times people followed mystical rituals and superstitions, and also practiced ancestor worship. Then, as in large part today for the Chinese, showing respect for one's ancestors is a fundamental rite of honor. The belief was that if a suitable grave site were chosen and properly cared for, you would be greatly blessed by that ancestor. The perfect geographical location was chosen; for example, on a beautiful hillside with a meandering brook nearby. Great care was taken so the grave faced the proper compass direction. Often, the living would become obsessed with beautifying their ancestors' graves to the neglect of daily activities! This practice is termed "Yin House," meaning "care for the deceased," and was the beginning of Feng Shui.

Founded on centuries of Yin House style, around the first century this primitive form of Feng Shui developed into "Yang House" style, where principles learned from the care of grave sites were applied to the living, material world.

Feng Shui was first documented about 200 B.C., just before the Chin dynasty. This was also about the time China, which was coined from the Chin family name, was "discovered" by the western world. Each succeeding dynasty in China's history influenced the development of Feng Shui. The social, political, and cultural emphasis of each dynasty's reign form the 3,000 years of China's elaborate history, and a vast number of Feng Shui concepts. Consequently, Feng Shui is a multifaceted topic, and its practice today uses the most commonly accepted principles.

FENG SHUI BRANCHES

Two principal branches have existed in Feng Shui since the ancient Yin House style, carrying over to the Yang House style, and to modern Feng Shui practice. What Feng Shui is truly about is understanding these two branches.

One is the Luan Tou Pai, "Natural Landmark Branch," which is concerned with geographical location and direction. In other words, Luan Tou Pai evaluates the actual physical structure, its placement, and its proximity to all else. The "school of forms" and "compass school" are founded in the Luan Tou Pai. They do not use "tools" or "cures" to mystically alter the Qi. They evaluate the exterior geographical location, and the room layout and interior structures.

A Luan Tou Pai Feng Shui master also looks for natural forms bearing resemblance to shapes that hold special meaning. A "dragon line" refers to a shape that creates a curving flow of Qi. Rivers, streams, mountain ranges, roads, and streets create that kind of form. A "tiger" refers to a monolithic form depicting solidity and strength. Thus, the Luan Tou Pai master would search for a solid "tiger" hill to build his business near, or a river to build his home on the curved "dragon's belly" bank.

In Luan Tou Pai, the main focus is finding the perfect location. Then, changing the Feng Shui can be done by the physical alteration of the environment. This would entail modification of the landscaping or reconstruction of the inside or outside of the structure. Practitioners of this style have argued for centuries that theirs is the most powerful form of Feng Shui because it is the most substantial and permanent.

The other branch, Li Qi Pai, "Regulating Qi Branch," is concerned with the quality of the Qi. A Li Qi Pai Feng Shui master will look at the same hill that the Luan Tou Pai master has seen, but instead searches for signs of good Qi. He will examine the abundance of plant and animal life. Abundant life means

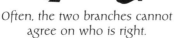

Often, the two branches cannot agree on who is right.

63

abundant Qi. Li Qi Pai masters will use many methods to alter and improve the Qi by either the use of "tools" or "cures," or with mystical rites and ceremonies. They follow the premise that imagery can alter the quality of the Qi. The Li Qi Pai practitioner would not move a wall as a Luan Tou Pai practitioner might do, but would place a "cure" there to accomplish a similar energetic effect. Li Qi Pai followers argue that their branch of Feng Shui is more effective because their use of tools and energetic cures does not entail physical alteration. Feng Shui corrections are therefore less costly and easier to apply.

Almost all practitioners of modern Feng Shui use theories from both branches. Both branches focus on the exterior and interior Feng Shui. But modern Feng Shui practitioners, especially those from a Western background, tend to lean toward Li Qi Pai, and they often mistakenly neglect the entire surroundings, and tend to focus on the interior Qi only.

We want to emphasize that neither branch is better than the other. Centuries of Feng Shui history have not brought a resolution to that argument, and neither can we. What is important to recognize is that there are times when altering the physical environment is the best way to improve the Qi flow. In other circumstances, placement of a meaningful tool can be an effective way to achieve the same effect. Your wisdom and intuition can help you choose the most appropriate form of Feng Shui.

CHAPTER 6: DESIGN AND DIRECTION

方位
設計

CREATIVE AND CORRECT INTERIOR DESIGN

To improve the interior Feng Shui you may just have to hang a wind chime. Then again, you may find yourself faced with the possibility of extensive reconstruction to effectively improve the Feng Shui. Wouldn't you like to avoid the second choice? Still, the architectural anatomy is the most permanent, the most influential, and should be the first thing evaluated: placement of walls, beams, room location and dimensions, doors, windows, ceilings, and stairways. The general decor is the easiest to change and should be dealt with after correcting the basic structure of the building. Often though, the most effective and permanent Feng Shui improvements to the architectural anatomy involve reconstruction.

Fortunately, you can save yourself money, time, and headaches by creatively using a Feng Shui cure or tool to effectively make corrections to the architecture. In other words, you can manipulate the decor to improve architectural faults. You may not need to hire a contractor to widen a narrow room. You can make the correction by hanging a large mirror on one wall to give the room visual depth and create the illusion that it is square, which is the most desirable and balanced shape in Feng Shui. A tiny, dark living room could be made larger and brighter by knocking out a wall to an adjacent room and adding windows. Or as an alternative, you could use light, paintings, and careful furniture rearrangement to better suit the space.

The decision to reconstruct or to use appropriate Feng Shui tools to make a correction is a judgment call based on the desired effect and the severity of the adverse Qi situation. Will the placement of a Feng Shui cure be effective enough to make a difference? A tiny living room may be acceptable without reconstruction. Then again, it might make all the difference in the world to add on extra square footage and install a skylight to bring sunlight into the room. Reconstruction is the only viable solution in many cases, especially when the situation has extremely detrimental Qi or is difficult to correct using a Feng Shui tool.

The lighting, color, decorations, furniture, and appliances are the easiest and least costly to change, and lend themselves to our creativity. Human nature is such that we become accustomed to our immediate environment. If required, we are able to adapt to even the worst conditions! We need to reexamine our living and working space with the eyes of Feng Shui, and notice the flow of Qi and how it affects us. Remember, you may have come to take your space for granted, so look for the obvious.

A dark, neglected corner could be made more usable by installing a bright light. A catch-all area could be made more appealing by rearranging the furniture. Climbing a closed-in, dreary stairway day after day may eventually create negative feelings. You may begin to feel your whole life is a heavy burden, or you might feel unable to accomplish even simple tasks. Painting the stairway a bright color and installing more lights will uplift your spirits as you climb. You will feel inspired to ascend to greater heights! A small room could be made to feel larger by a painting of a sprawling seascape. In a business, a couch could be strategically placed so it is the first thing a guest sees upon entering. Wouldn't this hospitable touch immediately make him feel welcome, and consequently more likely to become a good client?

The first moment you step into your home should initiate feelings of comfort and uplifting energy. Ideally, the main entrance should open into the family or living room; these spaces are Qi reservoirs, the gathering places of the family—the heart of the home. The mental impression you receive the moment you arrive home profoundly influences your psyche. If you find yourself drawn to a particular room in your house, look at the Feng Shui—what is it that appeals to you, and how does it affect your mental attitude?

Many homes in the United States are designed with less-than-perfect interior Feng Shui. More often than not, the entrance used most leads directly into the kitchen. After a period of time, the subtle message is reinforced that food is the first comfort we receive when we get home—so we spend a lot of time gazing into the refrigerator. Could this architectural design be a reason for all the concern about weight gain in the United States?

Also, many homes are designed so that you come into the house through the garage entrance. Most often this leads right into the laundry or utility room. There are several things you can do to correct this undesirable "first moment you arrive Qi." First, be flexible. Do not habitually use the garage entrance every time. Enter often through the front door, to provide yourself a better first impression. Second, enhance the garage entry area. Keep it clean and neat—no dirty laundry hanging everywhere! Also, Feng Shui tools can bring good Qi to an otherwise less-than-uplifting garage-style entrance.

THE GREAT OUTDOORS, THE GREATEST INFLUENCE: EXTERIOR DESIGN

As you study Feng Shui your first impulse might be to go out and buy a crystal to hang near your cash register. But wait, let's consider the great outside world first! Actually, the exterior Qi has far more influence on the dwelling than the interior Qi does, and a Feng Shui reading should begin on the journey to the site. Natural landmarks such as visible hills, mountains, valleys, and bodies of water, as well as manmade structures, all have a profound effect on the location of your home. Remember the old saying that history repeats itself? It is also important to investigate the historical significance of your suburb, neighborhood, and the house.

Mountain

Mountaintops are considered holy places that provide special protection; in many cultures, including the Chinese, people often climbed to the top of a chosen mountaintop to pray because it is considered a holy place. Mountains, hills, or buttes all have profound influence on Feng Shui. The view of a round-topped, beautiful mountain from the right of the main entrance is thought to be perfect placement in Feng Shui to bring great luck and protection. A house nestled in a group of mountains with the front door facing a gentle sloping valley is also perfect placement. The house is "nestled and protected" because it is sheltered on three sides. It is not best to have a house on the top of a single dominant hill or mountain. It would be hit by strong wind, and it is a sitting duck for lightning. The house is more vulnerable to the elements. Over time, that subtle "Qi message" of feeling vulnerable could influence the mental attitude of the residents. They may begin to feel insecure in relationships or finances. But if there are several rolling hills or mountains harmoniously blending together, then a house on top of one of them is acceptable.

Mountains that are pointed and steep, forming a craggy, harsh shape, are less desirable to build a house near than soft, rolling mountains or hills. Many cultures have placed great meaning on the shapes of mountains. The Chinese believe mountains are especially lucky if they resemble certain animals or objects. Building a house near the "head"

This mountain has a luck shape: a resting dragon.

of a "tiger" or "dragon" mountain can bring good luck. It would be considered meaningful if the mountain formed the shape of a buddha: it was believed to bestow heavenly protection.

Bodies of Water

A house built near a river would be either adversely or positively influenced depending on where it is in proximity to it. This rule was derived from observing the ebb and flow of bodies of water. Those living on the outside curve (dragon's back) of a river were flooded regularly; those on the inside curve (dragon's belly) benefited from better fishing. A house should be located a reasonable distance away from a body of water with the entrance facing it, if possible. A lake is good to live near, as long as the water is not stagnant or dirty. A pond on a property is considered good Feng Shui—water represents abundance. A swimming pool

A winding form such as a meandering river or curving road
is called a dragon line. The safest place is on the belly, and
riding on the back is the most dangerous.

is considered essentially the same as a pond. Again, the water must be fresh and clean, otherwise the effect will be detrimental. A view of the ocean from your home or business is considered to bring fortune. Is it a coincidence that the wealthy prefer to build their villas with an ocean view?

Valley

If a valley is located near the back of a house it may cause the residents to feel "caught in a rut," but a valley just a short distance from the front of the house would help "hold the good Qi for prosperity." You do not want to build a house in the bottom of a valley—it would be more likely to be damaged or even washed away in a heavy rainstorm. Consequently, over time the natural Qi flow of that valley would have the same adverse energetic effect, which may lead to emotional or financial equivalents of what is possible on the environmental level.

Earth or Soil

The Qi derived from the land is the living foundation and your connection to the Earth. This "Earth Qi" nourishes the dwelling much like it would nourish a plant. The soil should be rich and have abundant foliage. Check the lot on which the dwelling sits, and even expand your view into the surrounding neighbors' yards. Everything should be green and healthy. Large trees are favorable as long as they don't totally dominate the house or block the natural flow of Qi. If greenery is dead or unhealthy it should be immediately replaced. Colorful flowers are a wonderful enhancement and bring happiness.

Animals

There should be noticeable activity from the animals, birds, or pets that live in the neighborhood, such as birdsong when you awaken. The Chinese believe that the hummingbird brings good luck, but will only come around when the Qi is good. They also believe that deer are a good sign, bringing prosperity. People intuitively feel it is special to be visited by raccoons, foxes, or other wildlife (skunks excepted!). If no animals or birds are present, then the Feng Shui is probably not good. Of course, there is an exception to this if you live in the inner city where there is little to support wildlife.

Neighbors

Check the general disposition of the neighbors, and ambience of the neighborhood. If the other houses are neat, have well-kept yards, and the neighbors are generally happy, it is a place you would like to live. It is a good idea to spend time in a neighborhood at various times of the day before you decide to move there. If you hear quarreling as you stroll by your potential neighbors, it is obviously not something you want to live near! If you learn that your neighbors are always having accidents, many unusual illnesses, fires, or bizarre bad luck, then it is a sign that something is not right.

Elements

The most obvious and dynamic effects we feel are those from the elements. Traditionally in Feng Shui, the effects of weather from a particular direction determined the direction a house or business should face. It was considered bad if the entrance to a medical clinic faced north or northeast, because in northern China the cold winter winds would blast in from the north bringing yellow dust. Thus it was practical to avoid the "evil northern winds" by considering the direction the dwelling faced. A south-facing dwelling could benefit from refreshing breezes in the summer and good ventilation. Obviously, not every building can be constructed to face in a particular direction, but observe the flow and effect of the elements on your home or business—is it exceedingly hot, cold, or damp from exposure to the elements?

Sunshine is vital for life and enhances our disposition. Studies have proven that there is a higher suicide rate in places where there is considerable cloud cover, and also during the shortened days of winter. It has been shown that bright light can waylay the depression caused from lack of sunshine. On the other hand, climates other than sunny ones may be preferable, depending on your personality. Many people love a blustery, cloudy day. We cannot always have sunshine, and we need diversity in weather to survive. This is natural, of course, and the most balanced climate is what suits you. But it is preferable to have some bright light to balance the Yin nature of darkness. Light is a desirable enhancement for businesses, a possible exception being the dining area of a sophisticated restaurant.

Manmade Structures

The exterior also includes manmade objects: adjacent dwellings, roads, bridges, playgrounds, graveyards, or other structures such as telephone poles, statues, or parking lots. These things affect the dwelling according to their function, or purpose, and how the flow of Qi is affected by them. For example, if a house is too close to a graveyard the residents may be adversely affected. You should not be superstitious or frightened of a graveyard, but practically speaking it is a place of rest and decay, and its Qi is opposite that of a growing family. Also, the Chinese believe that you don't want a house placed in close proximity to a temple or church. This is because funeral services are traditionally held in these places and great sadness is expressed, which may adversely affect your emotions.

In large part our urban world is composed of manmade things. There is much to consider in modern Feng Shui about how these things affect Qi flow. If a large pole, structure, or tree is located directly in line with the main entrance and is in close proximity, the natural flow of Qi would be obstructed. A street is active with traffic, the Qi flows along with a certain speed and sensibility. The Qi flow from a street is similar to that of a stream or river. They should be considered essentially the same when evaluating Feng Shui, except that streets may have much more activity.

74

General Flow of Qi

Qi tends to flow along the same pathways as other things, such as water, wind, or traffic. Qi also follows the rule of gravity (actually, gravity is a form of Qi). For example, a dwelling would be adversely affected if it were

This freeway is creating a "dragon line" of Qi flow. The best location to build a house or business is on the belly, or inside, of the curve.

overshadowed by a sheer cliff, or sitting very near a precarious ledge. The house under the cliff would be in danger of something falling on top of it, and the house near the ledge would be in constant danger of being swept over the side. Over a period of time the energetic effect from such placement would cause harm. The residents in the house under the cliff, for example, may be plagued with frequent accidents. A house placed at the end of a blind alley is the target at the end, and may suffer from the effects of fast flowing Qi. A main entrance should not sit lower than the street level; Qi flows much like water does, and adverse Qi from the street flows into lower areas—and maybe into your cozy living room! In the same vein, the plot a dwelling sits on should be lower in front than in the back. This reinforces the idea that a hill or mountain to the rear of the dwelling serves as protection from the elements.

In this modern age, power lines are conduits not only of actual energy but also of adverse Qi. Electromagnetic fields have been shown to cause illness and even cancer in children. Are there huge power lines close to your home? Are you sleeping eight hours a day with your head very near an outlet or other power source? What effects from Qi flow might we experience from exposure to these fields, let alone health problems? It is a good idea to have the electromagnetic fields measured in and around your home. Most power companies provide this service free of charge.

Signs and Warnings

Also be keenly aware of obvious bad omens. If you are looking at a house with a realtor and the key becomes stuck and the door can't be opened, maybe you should consider the meaning behind this event. If you enter a prospective home, turn on a light and it blows out at that moment, what could it mean, and how does it make you feel? You must trust your deeper intuition and try to discover the meaning behind a peculiar event. What impression or feeling would you have if you came across a dead bird directly on the pathway leading to the front door of a house you were thinking of buying? Look for subtle hints and omens, these clues mean something—they expose the "Qi field."

DIRECTION AND THE I-CHING/BA GWA

There are basically three major ways to influence Qi in an environment:

1. Creating harmonious Qi flow by altering or enhancing it directly or with tools.
2. Making placement changes by using rules of direction and mathematics.
3. Using image or concept to positively influence the psyche, thus making you less influenced by undesirable Qi (see Chapter 4: Six Levels of Existence Influencing Humanity).

A minimal explanation of the second concept, which primarily involves study of the "I-Ching" and "Ba Gwa," is necessary to convey Feng Shui theory and use of directions. We hope this section will spur you on to study the I-Ching, its application to Feng Shui, and Chinese thought. In our experience, advanced I-Ching theory used in Feng Shui can bring powerful results.

"Ba" means eight, "Gwa" means displayed symbols, and the "I-Ching" (pronounced ee jing) translated from Chinese means the Book of Changes. The theories associated with the Ba Gwa (eight different symbols with much meaning placed on each one) are the basic building blocks of I-Ching theory.

Various schools of Feng Shui practice have sprung up throughout Chinese history: the "Black Hat School," incorporating ritual and mysticism; the "Form School," which is based on environmental formations and auspicious shapes; and the "Fukien School" (Compass School) focusing on direction and numerology. The "Compass School" primarily focuses on principles derived from study of the I-Ching and Ba Gwa, but all practitioners of modern Feng Shui use these constructs. The Compass School uses a compass called the loupan, but it is not the kind you would take on a hiking trip (see illustration, page 60). The loupan is a sophisticated tool used to decipher the best direction and location, according to the I-Ching/Ba Gwa.

The theory of Ba Gwa/I-Ching and direction in Feng Shui is very intriguing; however, it is also complicated and too broad a subject to cover in a single text such as this. The ideas are logical, and interrelated on many levels—it is captivating to study. It is quite worthwhile to pursue the Ba Gwa/ I-Ching more completely, and we hope to offer it as a specific topic in another publication. A brief summation is necessary, however, because the Ba Gwa and direction is a primary maxim of Feng Shui, used to some degree in all schools.

The I-Ching was written in China thousands of years before the birth of Christ, and has been a guide for leaders and scholars throughout Chinese history. It is believed by many of our contemporaries to be the vehicle for understanding the patterns of change that govern all life and occurrences. Fundamentally, it is a group of universal theories that explain the passage of time, changes in the seasons, movement, and astrology. It strives to explain how all things in the universe interact and affect one another, and ultimately how humans are affected by these changes. An adept student of the I-Ching can predict (with some accuracy) what is going to happen to him in the future based on past information, mathematical calculations, and logical series of events.

The term "I-Ching" has many implications. "I" means

simple change, yet can also mean complicated change—everything in the universe changing at the same time, such as the symphony of the movement of stars. "I" in another expression means alternating change, such as day into night. Additionally, "I" means that universal laws are unchangeable. "I" also denotes no change, referring to God as the unchangeable central source—with all else revolving and evolving through change. Strange as it may seem, these apparently contradictory meanings are all correct within their particular context. Our purpose is not to confuse you, but rather to whet your appetite for the I-Ching: it is widely available in many languages and versions.

The I-Ching is extrapolated from the sixty-four hexagrams (six lines), which are derived from any two of the eight trigrams (three lines) stacked together. The Ba Gwa are the simple eight trigrams, the real "meat" of the I-Ching. The "Eight Directions" used in Feng Shui are derived from specific arrangement of the Ba Gwa. The Ba Gwa symbols are written as three lines expressed as either broken or straight in different configurations:

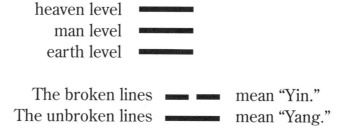

The I-Ching is based on the principle that everything in the universe exists in relationships of opposite expressions of duality. Yin and Yang are opposite states of a cycle existing in mutual opposition and dependence. They are interdependent in that one cannot exist mutually exclusive of the other: they define and create each other. Yin and Yang are also in a constant state of dynamic balance wherein either one adjusts to a relative level of the other. Traditional examples of Yin and Yang are fire and water, light and dark, morning and evening, and male and female. The Ba Gwa symbols are composed of these Yin or Yang lines, and the mathematical permutation of these two lines placed in three different positions creates eight unique possibilities.

The I-Ching/Ba Gwa is used in Chinese thought, Chinese medicine, philosophy, art, literature, and of course Feng Shui. The Ba Gwa is written primarily in two different forms for use in Feng Shui. One arrangement is the Fu-Xi Gwa, often used as a tool for protection (see page 97) and the other, the Wen-Wang Gwa, used to diagram the eight directions in Feng Shui (see page 81).

When using the directional Ba Gwa arrangement (Wen-Wang Gwa) in Feng Shui, it is aerially superimposed, using the main entrance of the room, house, or plot of land as the direction North (north by the compass is not used in this instance).

Each Ba Gwa symbol expresses a direction, and each Gwa also has a myriad of meaning attached to it. Each Gwa also corresponds and relates to the other Gwas as determined by their meaning and relative position. Following is a brief explanation of the eight Gwas according to their application in Feng Shui.

The Wen-Wang Ba Gwa Is the Most Common
Arrangement Used For Qi Enhancement Location

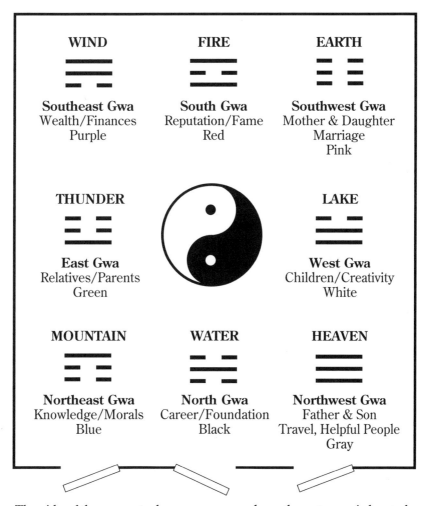

WIND

Southeast Gwa
Wealth/Finances
Purple

FIRE

South Gwa
Reputation/Fame
Red

EARTH

Southwest Gwa
Mother & Daughter
Marriage
Pink

THUNDER

East Gwa
Relatives/Parents
Green

LAKE

West Gwa
Children/Creativity
White

MOUNTAIN

Northeast Gwa
Knowledge/Morals
Blue

WATER

North Gwa
Career/Foundation
Black

HEAVEN

Northwest Gwa
Father & Son
Travel, Helpful People
Gray

The side of the property, house, or room where the entrance is located is the North Gwa; the door can be located anywhere along this side.

K'an

The North Gwa represents water, which corresponds to career, or the foundation inherited by one's ancestors. This could be seen as wealth, prestige, family name or title, and so on. It is expressed as the color black. An appropriate tool that could be placed in this area would be a plant or a painting/photo of bamboo, symbolizing growth and accomplishment. An indoor water fountain is also appropriate.

Chi'en

The Northwest Gwa means heaven. It is the most Yang Gwa, composed of three unbroken lines. Male is Yang by nature, therefore it is associated with relationships between yourself and your father and eldest brother, or meaningful times in your father's life. In Chinese culture the eldest brother is respected much like the father is. This Gwa symbolizes travel. It also represents helpful people. A photo of a father, or father figure, could be placed in this area, or photos of people who are helpful to you. A plant could also represent the growing efforts of helpful people.

Tui

The West Gwa, symbolizing the lake, is the relationship between yourself and your children or those people who take the role of children to you. It also represent creativity. Its color is white. A fish tank or a wind chime are good tools to place in this area. This would be the ideal part of your house to do your creative work: your studio, office, or den. It is the children's Gwa, the perfect location for a child's bedroom.

The Southwest or Earth Gwa represents the relationship between yourself and your mother and sisters. It also represents the marriage relationship. This is the most Yin Gwa, composed of three broken lines, thus its meaning relates to female, which is Yin in nature. Its color is pink. Something representative of love, such as a romantic painting, or even a mated pair of lovebirds, could be placed in this area to bring that energy.

The South Gwa, which means fire, represents your fame or reputation, position, or self-earned respect. It is expressed as the color red. Something meaningful in relationship to your profession could be placed in this corner, such as your law library if you are an attorney. This is the perfect area to hang your credentials or diplomas.

The Southeast or Wind Gwa symbolizes your financial power as expressed in ownership of property, wealth, or invested funds. Its color is purple. Appropriate tools to place here would be a coin collection, crystal ball, decorative light or chandelier, or small decorative fountain. A place of business may want to have their safe box in this Gwa position, or the book-keeper could have her desk in this area of the office.

Chên

The East Gwa, which represents thunder, is symbolic of your relationship to your family, especially the relationship between you and your parents. It could also include those who are your superiors or mentors. Its color is green. This area could be enhanced by placing a photo here of your parents, your in-laws, or a photo from a family reunion.

Kên

The Northeast Gwa means mountain, and represents your intelligence, education, accumulation of wisdom, and acquisition of moral standards. Blue is the color associated with this Gwa. A meaningful credential could be placed here such as a diploma to represent your education, or a religious/spiritual icon representing your morals and integrity.

When using the directional Ba Gwa, objects that symbolize protection, enhancement, or even a particular color can be placed in a desired Gwa position (see Chapter 7—Tools and Cures). However, the entire house should be balanced and harmonious, otherwise it will create confusion. Any intended enhancement of Feng Shui will be nullified. In other words, do not place a fish tank in each of the eight positions in your house. It will most certainly be strange, and will create disharmony and imbalance, eventually causing you to "drown" in a sea of problems! When altering Feng Shui, be careful not to succumb to the contemporary concept that "If a little is good, then a lot is better."

As you probably have figured out by now, the I-Ching/Ba Gwa has other uses in Feng Shui besides determining eight room positions. For one, the most advantageous direction the house faces, and what rooms of the house are most compatible to you, can be determined from your year of birth. Traditionally, use of I-Ching and Feng Shui overlap, making for vast gray boundaries, which is typical of Chinese thought. In some ways, I-Ching and Feng Shui are merely extensions of each other, because both are ancient, broad-based systems stemming from the same common roots.

Feng Shui masters use the Ba Gwa/I-Ching as part of a reading only. A few styles of Feng Shui are usually applied. Consideration is given other things which affect the Qi, such as personal relationships and history. It can be mind-boggling to construct an accurate reading! That is why we suggest hiring a professional Feng Shui consultant if a property or dwelling may entail a substantial investment. A professional consultation will prove to be most accurate and beneficial in the long run.

Credit for the Ba Gwa information in this chapter goes to Professor Lin Yun, Feng Shui master and leader of Tibetan Black Hat Buddhism in the Western world. He has compiled this information into an easily understood form from the classical Chinese I-Ching texts; and his interpretations are widely used in contemporary Feng Shui.

This meandering river has excellent Feng Shui because the Qi flow of the water is harmonious, and the water is so clear and fresh that the bottom can be seen.

Living near an ocean is excellent Feng Shui, but you should not live too close because the powerful movement of the ocean Qi could be overwhelming. Beach front is good, as is other varied terrain. However, the coastline here is a little too rocky to be considered perfect Feng Shui.

This highly reflective pond has excellent Feng Shui. Water reflection multiplies the good Qi. The round shape of the pond and its little island is harmonious with the water and resembles a coin. It is filled with fish, favored by wild water-fowl, and surrounded by beautiful trees.

Adverse Qi from the street would flow into this building because the entrance is lower than street level. The Qi flow is aimed directly at the door from the intersection. Qi flows much like water does, and behaves like gravity . . . actually, water movement and gravity movement are forms of Qi.

The harsh Qi flow from this straight street could cause cars to crash into this divider. The "keep right" sign may have been put up because this very thing happened.

Can you see the "secret arrow of Qi" created by the corner of the house in front? It is bad Feng Shui if your house is in close proximity to a sharp corner aimed your way, especially if there is nothing blocking the path of Qi.

87

Structures designed with arches are prominent in both Eastern (above) and Western (right) architecture. The shape is good Feng Shui because it is a balanced design promoting the smooth flow of Qi. Also, archways are structurally the strongest weight-bearing form.

88

These graceful walkways have curved pathways that move Qi gently and peacefully: a walkway in Peking's Forbidden City (right), the organ pavilion in Balboa Park, San Diego (bottom). Both have arches and rounded columns expressed in their architecture, preferred forms in Feng Shui.

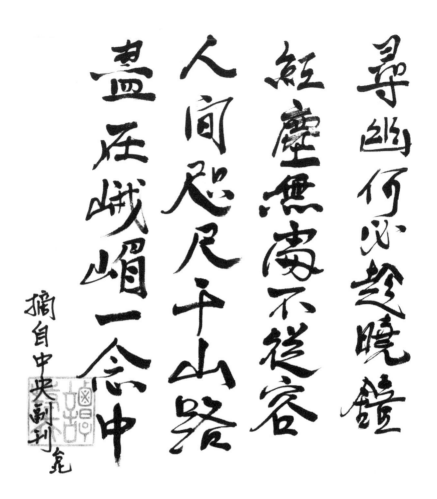

尋幽何必趁晚鐘
紅塵無處不從容
人間咫尺千山路
盡在峨嵋一念中

摘自中央副刊

*If you seek peace, it is not necessary
to follow the sound of the morning bell
because peace is everywhere. In your life
you can take the easy path, or scale a
thousand mountain roads, it all depends
on the truth that is in your heart.*

CHAPTER 7: TOOLS AND CURES

As you dabble in the basics of Feng Shui and start making changes in your surroundings, you will naturally find yourself faced with choices—because usually, there is more than one way to correct Feng Shui. There are fantastic stories about famous masters who used creative and innovative solutions to correct the Feng Shui. As a beginner you only have to tap your creativity to do the same thing. In modern society there are more decorating choices than ever before. Practically speaking, you have more options available to your creative forces than the ancients did. Your decor does not have to be Chinese for Feng Shui to work, so you can come up with unique ideas to fit your personal needs and tastes.

Depending on the situation, correcting Feng Shui may include direct alterations, such as reconstructing part of a building. Because of the realities of expense, inconvenience, personal interest, or architectural structure limitations, it might become too costly and impractical for many people to make such drastic changes. Fortunately, there are methods of applying Feng Shui that may save you from having to move from a home, or the headache and expense of a major reconstruction project.

You can employ various "tools" or "cures" traditionally used in Feng Shui to balance, improve, or modify Qi. These tools add a dimension of enjoyment to Feng Shui, because they give you a creative edge in the ability to improve your space. You can make improvements in an indirect way, as opposed to such direct methods as reconstructing an entryway. Because of the versatility of these tools, Feng Shui is flexible and accommodating, yet can still have a dramatic effect on the environment. You might decide to hire a five-man construction team to rebuild the entryway to your house. Doesn't it sound much simpler, not to mention less costly, to place a meaningful Feng Shui tool there to accomplish a similar energetic effect?

The traditional Feng Shui tools and cures described in this chapter are commonly used because of the mental images projected by our association with them, or the historical meaning that has been placed on them. We will explain what these tools and cures are, their use in Chinese history, as well as modifications for contemporary use in a creative, tasteful manner.

We have divided the tools into two general categories according to their use:

Tools for Protection against negative influences or bad Qi; essentially, to fend off the adverse Qi of something or someone.

Tools for Enhancement to upgrade low-energy places, or for situations that need special reinforcement or help.

TOOLS FOR PROTECTION

Curtain, Wall, or Door

Curtains or doors are used to block negative Qi or undesirable influences from invading a specific area. Curtains are hung in windows for privacy, but can be used in other places as well. A curtain can partially block an area to make it appear smaller, or set boundaries for privacy. A valance can create an illusion of an archway, a desirable shape that can visually reduce a tall doorway. A closed door can block or reroute the Qi flow. If the bedroom door is directly facing the bathroom door, it would be desirable to keep either door shut at all times. Actually, the bathroom door should be kept closed as much as possible because the bathroom is a place of elimination. Bathrooms are not evil places; it is just best to control the adverse Qi that their use naturally produces. Many houses built over 80 years ago had an outhouse separate from the main house, which is the ideal place for it. But this is an impractical arrangement for modern buildings, so be aware of the "bathroom Qi" so that it does not adversely affect you.

A wall can protect privacy, reroute the flow of Qi, or provide a sense of security, even though it may not provide actual physical protection. A wall can be built to reroute what is termed "straight arrow Qi." It is preferable to have Qi meander back and forth harmoniously and peacefully in a more circular motion. Very few things in nature are aligned in the straight, unbroken lines we find in modern architecture. Qi flow is accelerated by such pathways. This kind of energy is harsh and disruptive. "Straight arrow Qi" can sweep away good elements, much as a hurricane-type wind might, leaving the space energetically void.

Suppose you have a dangerous-appearing view from your auto body shop—let's say you are near a railway station with a view of oncoming trains. Building a thin wall to block your view would provide peace of mind. On a more practical note, if your house were very close to the bottom of a precipitous hill, a strong wall near the foundation would protect it from mud slides, falling objects, and earthquakes. It would provide both practical protection as well as peace of mind.

Fan

The fan has an interesting place in Chinese history. The fan, along with the stick, sword, and knife, are classical weapons in the martial arts, particularly Kung Fu. Although the sword and knife are used more aggressively, and the Chinese sword is light and easy to carry, traditionally the fan is the weapon of choice for women. It was customary for women in ancient China to always carry a fan—for many reasons. It was used to fan oneself, of course, but also served as a modest cover. It was proper etiquette for a woman to cover her teeth with a fan when she laughed, or her face if she flushed with color from embarrassment or emotion.

Martial arts forms created exclusively for the fan are beautiful and graceful. A weapon fan would be made of metal, with its edges sharpened. The artist would flick it

Proper way to display a fan for protection. The red tassel is an added enhancement.

open and closed as she performed the movements. A snap of the wrist could cut an opponent with its wide edge; or closed, serve as a stick to jab or strike. The fan is used as a protective symbol in Feng Shui because of all these traditional uses. It is a popular design element of ancient and modern Chinese art and architecture. If you feel unsafe at night, and have difficulty sleeping, a decorative fan can be placed above the head of your bed. This powerful and beautiful symbol can provide a feeling of comfort, as well as dispel negative or depressive Qi.

Mirror

Mirrors are perhaps the most versatile and powerful of the tools used in Feng Shui, and are used both for enhancement and protection. A mirror produces a perfect reflection: it returns the image back to its source. A huge building that overshadows and overwhelms yours, a funeral parlor in close proximity, or other ominous or threatening views naturally have negative effects. A mirror facing that direction will reflect not just the image, but the detrimental Qi produced by it. A mirror can be hung above a door facing a discourteous, malicious neighbor. Then, every time he scowls in your direction with a criticizing attitude, he will be confronted by his own negative energy.

Regarding placement, with the exception of a narrow hall or foyer, never decorate with two mirrors facing each other, in a bedroom or any other room. The images generated by facing mirrors are infinite! The production of such energy quickly unsettles the mind. A mirror should not be facing the foot of the bed, so that when you sit up or look around you are immediately confronted with your reflection. This feeling of "many presences in the room" can eventually lead to anxiety and insomnia.

Ba Gwa Symbol

The Ba Gwa in Chinese culture is a symbol of perfect balance. Refer to Chapter 6 for a complete explanation and history of Ba Gwa. It has a solid and defending character because of its historical and fundamental meaning associated with the I-Ching. The Fu-Xi Gwa style is considered to be its most perfectly balanced expression, and it is the style most commonly used in Feng Shui symbolism (see page 97). The Fu-Xi Gwa is traditionally hung above the busiest door in a household to protect the residents against the effects of negative invading energy. Often a small mirror or a Yin/Yang symbol is in the center of the Fu-Xi Gwa to provide more balance and protection.

Sword or Knife

Of all the Feng Shui tools, weapons are the most powerful expressions of self-defense and protection. Weapons are

There are many ways to configure the Ba Gwa. One unusual arrangement was even credited to Confucius. The Fu-Xi Gwa, drawn thousands of years ago, is most often used as a symbol of protection. The trigram arrangement is read from the inside out, and the trigram heaven should always be at the top. The center of the Fu-Xi Gwa is either a small mirror or a rendering of the Yin/Yang symbol.

used to defend oneself against attack, and thus they provide a sense of protection wherever they are displayed. This category also includes other traditional weapons of defense, such as fighting sticks or guns. Weapons should be displayed in a prominent place, usually on the living room or den wall. In the United States, guns are often used as decoration: the old Winchester hung above the fireplace on a ranch. Probably those who started this Western tradition were led by intuitive logic as well as practicality. The gun symbolized protection, and was easily accessible in an actual emergency.

There are some basic rules for displaying or hanging weapons in the home:

Do not hang a sword in a kitchen, as there are already many sharp objects (knives) there. The overabundance of sharp objects may possibly create verbal disagreements ("sharp tongues" is a good analogy of what may happen).

A knife or sharp weapon should not be displayed over the head of a bed or on the wall behind a couch. The subconscious mind is influenced more by visual perception than by reasonable logic. Anyone sitting or sleeping under a potentially dangerous object, such as a knife pointing toward them, would feel uneasy and tense.

Beads

Beads are used to separate or partition off an area, or to slow down the flow of Qi. If the study is meant to be private, then beads could be strung across the entry as a divider without closing off the room. This subtle yet effective tool serves to gently remind inquisitive guests that the area is off limits. Beads can also be used to slow down the flow of Qi in a space where it passes through too quickly, such as a house with a long straight hallway. The sound of the beads being pushed aside as one passes through them enhances their energetic function.

Wind Chimes or Bells

The effect of wind chimes is similar to that of beads, except they do not provide the barrier created by strung beads. However, wind chimes are more melodious to the ear. Sound is a very powerful tool in Feng Shui to influence mood, and the Qi. The musical tones serve as a conduit to disperse energy from anywhere they are heard. Wind chimes are most effective if hung in a draft which moves them. A wind chime can be hung in a long hallway to decelerate the flow of Qi. For example, squanderous spending in a household could be considered out-of-control Qi. The pleasant tones from chimes will adjust and temper the Qi, and may help bring the budget back under control. Bells are also tools of sound. Strung bells on a doorknob are a simple security device used by many retail shops to fend off any would-be thieves.

Sharp Object

A sharp-pointed object wards off invasive Qi much as a mirror does. A sharp-pointed object, however, is aggressive by nature—it is sharp, piercing, and projects out. You can aim a sharp object directly at the window or door of a person who invades your privacy, or otherwise causes unwarranted trouble. Actually, it is the most appropriate tool to fend off Qi from another sharply pointed object aimed your direction: for example, the corner of a roof which is at perpendicular angles, and in close proximity with your dwelling. This roof corner creates an aggressive energetic "arrow" aimed your way. Wouldn't this naturally instill an uncomfortable feeling over a period of time? Using a sharp-pointed object as a Feng Shui tool in a case like this can be compared to two people drawing their swords, equally matched for battle.

The sharp-pointed object is often used to balance a gentle, good-natured person against an overwhelming invasive force. This tool is especially effective when the person using the sharp object is the underdog in the situation; it gives him an energetic edge.

Heavy Object—Rock, Urn, or Statue

A large, heavy object is used to create a feeling of stabilization. Mass naturally has a pulling down, grounding energy. A heavy object can be used as a Feng Shui cure for a personal situation that you may feel insecure about. It can help you deal with the uncertainty of an unstable present or future. If you feel you are in a position to be fired any day from your job, or fear that you will come home one day and find your significant other left you (without reasonable cause), a heavy object will help you feel more "grounded." A heavy rock, planter, or statue can be placed in your yard as decoration, or a big, flat rock can be used as a platform or deck to create the "heavy object" effect. Roman pillars create the same energetic "grounding" effect because they have such mass.

TOOLS FOR ENHANCEMENT

Wind Chimes or Bells

Wind chimes, bells, or other pleasant "noise-makers" are useful as Feng Shui tools not only for protection but for enhancement as well. The wind chime provides a cheerful energy because of its melodious, pleasant sound. It also reacts to light and air flow. These three things: air, light, and sound, are often manipulated in Feng Shui to enhance Qi. A wind chime can be hung wherever there is energetic weakness. A room in your house may have low energy—a corner of a room may seem unusable, uncomfortable, or furniture doesn't go well there. A wind chime can be hung in that area to bring uplifting Qi. A wind chime can be used to "call in good luck." Often, retail stores that are Chinese-owned, have a wind chime near the door to bring in customers.

Crystal Ball

Crystal balls have traditionally been used for ritual practices in Buddhism, and are believed by many to be endowed with special powers. A crystal ball should be highly reflective and refractive, with a many-faceted surface. The

sparkling, moving rainbow of light cast by a crystal ball strengthens the Qi in an area. If you discover that a particular corner of your house is dark, or that it is a lifeless dead-end, you can hang a crystal ball from the ceiling in that location. One woman purchased a beautiful cut crystal after she learned a little about Feng Shui, and hung it in the financial corner of her living room (see Chapter 6 regarding corners of a room). Three weeks later she won over $3,000 in a lottery game. It would be conjecture to say the crystal was why she won the prize money. It could just as well have been a nice decoration for the woman, and the money was a coincidence. In any case, Feng Shui does have an influence on the environment—it may be subtle, or dramatic. Most likely the crystal provided mental support to the woman rather than rendering mystical powers . . . but those things can't be measured, can they? So who really knows?

Light

Everybody knows that light uplifts the spirit and casts out darkness, whether physical, mental, or spiritual. Light is extremely important in Feng Shui, and is used for all the above reasons and is a primary cure to impart good energy. Light brings clarity and reveals truth, and enhances our mood as well. Light also can create the illusion of space. A square or rectangle is the ideal shape for a room or struc-

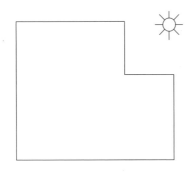

ture: it is a balanced form geometrically and for Qi distribution. If the layout of a particular house is "L" shaped, a light can be placed outside right where that missing corner would have been. Illuminating a missing area helps compensate for an imbalance caused from any unusually shaped structure.

Light can be extremely beneficial to a business if used properly. As a general rule, the brighter the better. Bulbs that are blown out should be immediately replaced. Light is especially important in businesses involving health care. A doctor, dentist, or acupuncture office must never have a poorly lit reception room. Darkness in these places easily breeds depression and anxiety in the psyche of those seeking relief for their ailments.

Color

Color has a profound effect on the psyche, and humans are almost exclusive in the ability to see color. Unlike most creatures, we depend on our sight more than any other sense. Different colors impart entirely different emotions and atmospheres. And color could even be conceived as a bridge between the physical and spiritual planes. Each color on the light spectrum vibrates at a specific frequency. Color creates a vibration on many levels, from the chemical reaction of the rods and cones in our eyes as it relays the message to our brains, to the vibration of red color attracting a honeybee to a flower. It could be said that Qi comes in different hues. Color is a powerful influence on the levels of feelings and image, and a powerful Feng Shui cure.

RED—is bright and exciting. Because it is such an alive, vibrant color, the Chinese believe that red is the luckiest of colors, bringing happiness, luck, warmth, fortune, and power. The Chinese bride will traditionally wear bright colors, especially red. Chinese parents will distribute bright red eggs to their children as gifts for certain holidays. When a happy couple announce the birth of their baby they will give red eggs to their friends, much like a new father in the United States will pass out cigars.

Reimbursements and gifts are usually presented in small, bright red envelopes called Hung Bao (Hung means red, and Bao means package or envelope). A monetary gift of appreciation or love is usually presented in a Hung Bao envelope. An individual repaying a generous loan will offer it as Hung Bao. Children are given money at Chinese New Year in a red Hung Bao envelope. Traditionally, Feng Shui readings are paid in a Hung Bao envelope, embraced in the "Black Hat School" as the "red envelope tradition." This signifies respect paid to the knowledge received.

In modern context, red has about the same universal flavor and meaning. Red is the favorite color for sports cars, a flashy attention-getter. Red can be worn for an occasion where you want to be noticed. You could wear a red tie or scarf for an important business meeting. Red is a powerful color that also expresses love and passion. Often, a woman will choose to dress in red to attract the opposite sex.

Red can be used to enhance an area or object; it is a wonderful accent color in decorating. Because it is the warmest color, it should not be dominant in the color scheme. It may create nervous excitement and may cause tempers to flare. A red ribbon tied around the pot of a plant accentuates the living Qi of the plant. Red tassels are often tied around flutes, strung bells, or fans to accentuate their positive effect.

DARK RED or PURPLE—is used to show, and to earn, respect. It is often considered even luckier than red because it symbolizes royalty, and positions of highest honor. It also portrays the qualities of wealth and good fortune. One may choose to wear purple to an important business meeting to command control, or have more presence. Purple should be used sparingly in decorating; it is best complemented with other colors such as gold.

GREEN—is a peaceful color that promotes feelings of new life and hope. You feel refreshed by the color green: it is the color of spring, and signifies good health. When in the market for purchasing property, check the natural earth Qi by how much greenery there is. Take into account the natural vegetation; a desert habitat will naturally be more sparse. If there are few plants, however, it is a clue that the property may not have the best Qi. A plot with rich soil that supports healthy flora is a good foundation for a house. You can enhance the exterior of your home with trees and a healthy lawn, but it is equally important to bring that life inside. Plants provide green color and life. If a room cannot support live plants, artificial can substitute, or use green as an accent color. Because green symbolizes life, it is a good color to wear if you feel depressed or have low energy. One gentleman, born the year of the sheep or goat, coincidentally liked the color green. He did horticulture as a hobby, and drove a bright green car. He said that green made him feel peaceful. Goats and sheep like green grass, so it was an appropriate color for this man.

YELLOW—is the color of the sunlight and of gold. Chinese associate the quality of longevity and power with yellow. Traditionally, the Chinese imperial palace colors were yellow or gold. During the Ching Dynasty, gold was reserved exclusively for palace royalty to wear. High-ranking Buddhist monks will wear orange or yellow robes, the yellow reserved to the highest rank, signifying greater respect. Yellow is a cheerful earth color, it is versatile as a wardrobe color or in decorating.

WHITE—the Chinese will wear white to express grief. In the West, black is for grieving, and is traditionally worn at funerals. In contrast, at a Chinese funeral, the immediate family will be dressed entirely in white. Both black and white have similar meanings of sadness or grief to the Chinese, but white is believed to be the deeper expression. This is because the attributes of white are blandness, sterility, and lack of character or flavor.

Because of its nature, white is an important color to use in decorating and fashion. It can be thought of as the palette for other colors. White also symbolizes purity and cleanliness, which is important in professions that require cleanliness, such as the food industry, a laundry or car wash, or the healthcare professions. Accent color is vital even in places where white is the dominant color. Because of its bland quality, many hospitals no longer require their staff to wear entirely white uniforms, sensing patients feel more comfortable when other accent colors are worn by their caretakers.

Color has a powerful effect on our psyche. An artist once painted his house entirely white, and the decor was white. It was completely white, devoid of any other color. This artist was always contracting one sickness after another. It was suggested that his sterile-white environment could be adversely affecting his health, and he should paint his front door red. The addition of healthy plants and colorful rugs offset the extreme lack of color and brought nourishing vitality to his environment.

BLUE—is the next least desirable color to white or black. Blue is a better color than white, but it is not a color of happiness, growth, or continued improvement. However, blue does mean stability and can be employed for that effect. Blue, a calming color, also instills feelings of serenity. But be careful not to use too much blue in your surroundings, as it may induce unhappiness. It can bring on the "blues," so to speak.

BLACK—is thought to express darkness, accidents, or bad luck. But black can also express depth of mood or thought. It is usually not good to use as a predominant color in design, but as an accent color. If black and white are used together in interior design, it is vital to add plants and sections of bright gold color as a complement. A woman who worked as an administrative assistant complained of a weak immune system. She was constantly catching any contagious illness that came her way. She suspected her living space might be at fault because her poor health coincided with a redecoration, so she had a Feng Shui reading done for her condo. It was of modern design, done entirely in black and white. It was suggested she add bright paintings with gold frames, big healthy plants, and provide additional lighting. The colors green and gold brought life into an otherwise color-bland environment.

PINK or PEACH—brings love and symbolizes feelings of purity and happiness. Those who would like to meet their significant other can wear pink. It was suggested by a Feng Shui master for one love-seeking gentleman to use pink bedcovers. He purchased an acceptably masculine lotus colored set. The Chinese term "Peach Blossom Qi" refers to the specific pink color of the blooms, and the quality of being extremely attractive to the opposite sex.

Mirrors

Mirrors have a special power in manipulating image. As you discovered in Chapter 4: Six Levels of Existence

Influencing Humanity, the level termed "image" is a quality that is easily manipulated in Feng Shui. Image can impart a strong impression in our minds, because what we experience through our senses, whether it is image or reality, is processed as reality in the subconscious mind. What do we think as we look at ourselves in the mirror? We trust what we see, disregarding the fact that we are viewing an image. Our thought process goes something like: "I am looking at myself, and gosh, my hair looks great," not "this image of myself implies that my hair looks great." Image is a powerful Feng Shui cure because it can easily alter our perception of reality.

In essence, mirrors create perfect images, linking what we perceive as reality and the unreal. Mirrors are masters of image, and in Feng Shui image is everything.

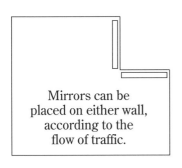

Mirrors can be placed on either wall, according to the flow of traffic.

Mirrors can enlarge or alter the visual space. You can make a room appear larger by mirroring one wall. Mirrors can make a space seem less confined. A house that is L-shaped is usually not preferable in Feng Shui; it is comparable to a square with a piece missing. A mirror placed on the wall where the piece is missing can visually balance the missing space.

A mirror can dramatically inspire a spatial change in a room. If a restaurant is rectangular, and much longer than it is wide, it can look out of proportion and narrow. Symmetrical geometric shapes create a balanced, secure atmosphere and are the most desirable shapes for buildings or rooms. A restaurant that is long and tunnel-like can be made to appear more square-shaped if mirrors are placed along the length of one long wall.

Mirrors also can "bring in a lucky view" from the ocean, a lake, or a beautiful garden. Water means wealth or abundance. An ocean view reflected in a mirror hung in your house brings in that wealth! Another common practice in Feng Shui is to place a mirror directly behind the cash register; this gives the image of "doubling your cash flow." In other words, mirrors reflect and enhance something desirable. Stove burners also represent wealth, and a mirror placed behind them gives the image of more burners.

A mirror can reflect what is happening behind you, thus providing a sense of security. If your back is to the main door at your workplace, you will naturally begin to feel uneasy: you cannot see who is entering or what is happening. If it is impossible to rearrange your work station, a mirror can be hung to provide you a view. When hanging a mirror, do not hang it lower than a person's average height. This "cut-off-head" effect when you look at the mirror may cause you to feel strange, and could give you a headache!

Plants

Plant life connects us with nature and surrounds us with positive life elements. Because plants have an upward-moving, light-seeking quality, they promote positive, uplifting energy. Healthy plants placed anywhere in your house or business increase the good Qi. Plants can counteract stagnant or lifeless energy in a room or corner. Plants placed on both sides of the front door of your business will help bring in clients.

Plants can also cover something undesirable: a dark area, corners, or an unwelcome view. Round leaf plants are best for enhancement. If the leaf shape resembles coins, the plant can be placed next to your front door to bring you riches! A plant with heart-shaped leaves can be placed in the marriage corner of your bedroom to bring your soul mate. A plant that has spiky and long, sharp leaves, such as aloe or cactus, can be placed on the corner of your balcony to provide a sense of protection. A cactus should not be placed too near the front door; its sharp personality tends to be uninviting.

Aquarium

An aquarium creates a beautiful image of abundant, flowing energy, and once again connects us with nature. It represents youth and activity, and promotes harmony. Watching the movement of fish in an aquarium is a meditative, peaceful activity—a great idea for a dental office waiting room. An aquarium is a powerful cure, bringing together water, which represents abundance; fish, which represent money; and color, bringing happiness.

If the living room is in the financial area of your house (see Chapter 6: Design and Direction) and is reserved only for rare occasions, then stagnant Qi from disuse will create an imbalance in your household. This may possibly lead to financial trouble. To balance the room, an aquarium and healthy plants could bring life and energy to this otherwise lifeless space. The room is "lived in" by these living things.

To benefit from the positive influence of an aquarium, it is important to keep it clean and stocked with healthy fish. A dirty aquarium is like a "stagnant dirty pool," and the intended positive influence will instead become detrimental. Goldfish represent financial power; they are the color of coins and flash in the light. The presence of goldfish in an aquarium creates the image for increasing wealth. There is a casino hotel in Nevada where an entire back wall in the reception area is a huge, beautiful aquarium. This Feng Shui cure attracts money.

Paintings/Ornaments

Your taste in artwork portrays your personality, or determines the energetic quality of your home or business. When

These Chinese decorations symbolize people working
together harmoniously (dragon figures), and the
making of money (coin-like shape).

you look at a painting, you learn about the artist's character, and about the person who chose it. In Feng Shui, paintings are used to create specific impressions to influence an area of the house. For example, a painting of bamboo can be placed in the "career corner" of the room (see Chapter 6 on areas of Ba Gwa). This painting will create the feeling of upward movement—of success and progress in one's career. A modern version of this idea might be a print of a Cape Canaveral liftoff. Subject matter for decoration really depends on your taste and decorating scheme. However, a review of traditional Chinese decor and painting can give you an idea of how Feng Shui works.

There are underlying themes present in virtually all Chinese artwork, and the objects in their paintings have specific—you could say cryptic—meanings attached to them. That is why certain flowers, plants, animals, and other objects are favored subjects in Chinese painting. Bamboo is often found in traditional paintings. It is straight and tall, so the Chinese regard it as an example of continued progress. The lotus also has specific meaning. When the lotus blossoms, the flower stands high above the level of the pond

water. Its beauty represents purity: it rises above the murky water from which it grows. The lotus symbolizes that you have the depth of character to uphold your standards and be unaffected by the surrounding corruption and immorality. A painting of lotus could be hung in the "morality/knowledge corner" of the room. The Chinese also like the chrysanthemum because the pronunciation of the character is similar to a character meaning "good fortune." A painting of a pair of mated birds projects the image of everlasting love. Such a painting can be hung in the "marriage corner" of the main room to protect and/or bring conjugal love. (Refer to Chapter 6 for

Ba Gwa areas of the room.)

Of course, paintings do not have to be specifically Oriental in flavor to have Feng Shui meaning. The sensitive person will select a painting with good Feng Shui because it "feels right." For example, a painting depicting tall pines has good Feng Shui. Evergreens especially depict growth and life because they are green year-round, and pines are among the oldest living things. The tall, straight pine gives the image of a long and prosperous life.

Decorative objects can be used in the same way paintings are. After learning a little about Feng Shui from his teacher, a martial artist placed a huge Chinese urn in the wealth corner of his living room. Into it he placed a kwon-do, a large Chinese weapon with a huge, hooked blade traditionally carried by soldiers on horseback. The image was striking and powerful. Shortly thereafter he inherited a large sum of money.

Moving objects move the Qi. A weather vane or whirly-gig can be placed to disperse harsh, fast-moving Qi from a nearby street. A retail store can place "moving gizmos" in their display windows to attract customers.

Bamboo

Bamboo grows tall and straight with a segmented stalk. This isignifies to the Chinese that a goal can be accomplished if taken step by step (in other words, with hard work and persistence). Sometimes, as added effect, red ribbons or tassels are tied to the bamboo. Red means happiness and brings good luck. Bamboo and red ribbons signify your good fortune will grow. Bamboo stalks can be hung verti-

cally, or at an angle, but should always be hung with the root end pointed toward the earth, and the leaf end upward. Flutes made of bamboo are often used for enhancement because music is uplifting to the spirit. They can be hung on exposed beams to provide an image of support, or on a wall behind the cash register to increase profits. The mouthpiece should be considered the "leaf end" if you are using a bamboo flute.

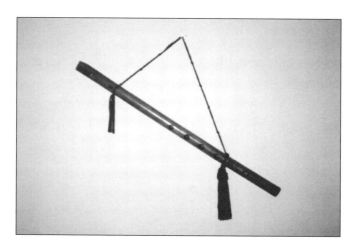

This decoration is made of and carved with a rendering of bamboo.

Fountain

Fountains move water. "Shui" means water, so of course a fountain is a major Feng Shui tool. Water means abundance or wealth, and historically this makes sense: civilizations always flourished around bodies of water. An office or a home that has a view of an ocean, lake, or river has good Qi. Fountains are used as landscaping tools in homes as well as businesses; they depict financial power. This is why even the huge, insipid concrete and glass buildings in corporate parks have a fountain near the front entrance—they want to show the world they have money.

Outdoor fountains can help break the path of adverse Qi

116

This fountain in Balboa Park, San Diego, serves to reroute
the flow of Qi from the traffic coming into the park.

flow. You can place a fountain between your house and an
offending building. The career section in your place of business is also represented as the element water. A fountain is
a perfect tool to place near the front door of your business to
enhance your income as well as your career.

This fish
statue foun-
tain is in front
of a grocery
store. It is
intended to
bring in good
fortune and
customers.

117

Water is a powerful cure, and it must be used carefully. If the image of water overpowers the building it is supposed to enhance, it will bring disaster instead of wealth and success. The Chinese saying, "Water can float the boat, but it can also sink it," explains what may happen. At one time a Tokyo bank decorated an entire wall with a huge, sheeting waterfall. It was impressive, but unfortunately, it was too overpowering. Within a short time, the bank literally and figuratively "went under" because there was too much water drowning out everything else, washing profits away!

Be creative. Using the traditional tools or cures gives you the added benefit of inheriting the historical integrity they possess. Feel free, however, to employ your own "tools" or "cures." The more meaning an object has for you, the more personal benefit (or power) you derive from it psychologically. A family heirloom has personal meaning; therefore, it has influence on you, and can be an appropriate Feng Shui tool. Use all Feng Shui tools and cures wisely, and apply them with the primary goal of creating a balanced and pleasing environment. If a fish tank is placed in a location that is inappropriate or in the way of regular activity, the intended effect will be nullified. If too many tools are placed in a location, then an atmosphere of confusion will pervade, detracting positive Qi, even causing a negative effect! The secret for success when manipulating Qi with Feng Shui tools is to use moderation and common sense to create harmony.

Feng Shui Photo Tour of the Famous Peking Forbidden City

The most impressive use of Feng Shui is in the famous Forbidden City, Peking, which was home to many generations of Chinese emperors. It was good luck to walk over the river running in front of the palace entrance. Only the emperor was allowed to walk over the center bridge.

Every palace has a stairway leading up to it, signifying loftiness. The more stairs, the higher the rank. The emperor's main palace (right) has the most stairs.

There are hundreds of sculptures in the Forbidden City. Both the turtle and crane mean good luck and long life, and are popular subjects in Chinese art.

In Chinese culture, as in many other cultures, the lion is a symbol of protection. Often an entrance is flanked by lion sculptures. A lion sculpture can also serve as the Feng Shui cure calling for a heavy, solid object, bestowing qualities of stability as well as protection.

Tens of thousands of pillars have been intricately carved with a relief of a dragon on each one. Dragons always mean good luck—of which the emperor must have had an abundance.

Three doors lined up in a row is generally considered
bad Feng Shui because it causes the Qi flow to accelerate—
and these doors are in the Forbidden City! The architects
maintained good Feng Shui, however, because a little
barrier was built at the bottom of each doorway which
had to be stepped over as one passed through. This
cure effectively slowed down the Qi flow.

Numerology is an important part of Feng Shui. The main palace in the Forbidden City (above) has nine guardian animals on the roof corners: nine being a number of ultimate fulfillment. The building (right) of lesser importance has only three guardian animals on its roof.

CHAPTER 8: TALES OF HAPPINESS

These are real people and real situations from Dr. Tan's experiences as a Feng Shui consultant. And yes, all the people in the stories gained great power, riches, and love beyond their wildest imagination! Actually, we made a real effort not to embellish the stories; only the names and/or the locations have been changed, to avoid the possibility of "Embarrassment Qi!"

The stories are arranged as you would do a Feng Shui reading: from the outside first, walking through the front door, then looking around inside. So sit back with this book, a cup of delicious tea and plate of almond cookies, and enjoy these humorous tales of happiness.

Heavy Iron Hat

A 45-year-old patient of mine suffered from chronic headaches. She was a thoughtful, soft-spoken woman who looked much younger than her years. She consciously evaluated her stress level, diet, and the physical surroundings whenever a headache began. She searched for correlations, but there were none. The headaches occurred inconsistently, and they were not related to weather or seasonal changes. Most of the time her headaches felt like there was a belt strapped tightly around her head, with a heavy iron hat pressing down on the top of her skull.

I treated her to control the pain and reduce the frequency of her headaches. Because there was nothing of significance in either Western or Chinese medicine that would cause such strange and intense headaches, I told her that a Feng Shui reading might be a good idea.

She lived in one of the oldest, well-known neighborhoods in San Diego. The homes were quaint, most of them built in the 1920s. Many of the older homes had been torn down and replaced by newer homes, condos, and apartments. But my patient's little house was in excellent shape, as were a number of the original homes, so she had no reason to rebuild. But, recently constructed four-story condo and eight-story apartment buildings began surrounding her house. These towering buildings dwarfed her house to such an extent that even sunshine could barely peek through! I then understood the nature of my patient's headaches. I explained her little house was dominated by

126

the overbearing, larger buildings. Her body was reacting to this suppressive Qi by having pressure headaches!

I offered two courses of action: she could sell the house and move; or, use a Feng Shui cure as a temporary solution. This would entail placing several sharply-pointed objects on her roof, each one aimed at the top of a big building.

My patient chose the second course of action. A few weeks after placing the pointed objects on the roof (I suggested pointed decorative chrome hubcaps from a junk yard), she reported a reduction in the occurrence and severity of her headaches. Two years later, she called to tell me she had moved, and was totally free of her miserable headaches.

Summary

Houses should be relatively the same size in a neighborhood to create the most harmonious environment. If a story is added to a house, the neighbors living close by usually aren't too happy if the house towers above and overshadows theirs. The view is often obscured, they may feel they have less privacy, and they feel generally "imposed upon." If your house is overshadowed by an imposing building, you can plant a row of trees or install a fountain between to block the suppresive Qi. You can also aim a pointed object their direction. Weather vanes or whirlygigs will do the trick and are cosmetically acceptable.

View of the Point

———•———

A woman who lived in a upscale beach area decided to redecorate the interior of the house herself. She asked for my input regarding Feng Shui as to furniture selection, color scheme, ornamentation, and so forth.

As I pulled my car around to park, I noticed hers was one of the nicer looking houses on the block. I could hear the surf as I rang the doorbell—she lived perhaps fifty yards from the ocean. She greeted me, offered me a cup of tea, and described her redecoration plans. We walked through the house, and I gave suggestions for all the rooms, halls, and entryways. She was delighted with the whole procedure—she found the suggestions practical and creative. Feng Shui also lent her a point of view about energetic influence in design. Being thorough, I asked to see the patio; surely she wanted to include it in the consultation. When she had to go find the patio door key, I realized she didn't use the patio very much. This surprised me, because a few minutes ago she told me how much she enjoyed the ocean view from there.

After she opened the door and I looked around, I instantly understood why she didn't like going out on the patio. I asked if she got along very well with her neighbor. The smile on her face instantly vanished. She told me in so many angry words exactly what she thought of her! After she calmed down, I explained that the corner of her neighbor's house was pointing directly at her patio. Not only that, it had large continuous corner windows on both sides. These two things together made for bad Feng Shui. The neighbor's pointed corner created a harsh, intrusive energy. The windows accentuated that effect, making it seem as if the neighbor were prying into her affairs (see illustration next page).

My client glared at the corner as if it were an adversary, but I assured her there was a solution: I suggested placing some tall plants on the patio to block the view of her neighbor's corner. I stressed that the entire building did not need to be blocked from view, just the pointed corner. I also told her to be creative and purchase some kind of object that had an obvious "point" on it, and attach it above the patio door. It should point directly at the neighbor's corner. This would deflect the intrusive Qi of the neighbor's point. Also, because the two points faced each other, the energy would be balanced on both sides.

She found a unique weather vane to serve as her "pointed object." She also blocked her view of the point with a couple of ficus trees. After changing things on her patio, she spent more of the summer there taking in the view and sun.

Summary

A pointed object projects adverse Qi toward anything that is directly in its pathway. This can be likened to someone pointing a drawn sword directly at you. A sword is threatening, it can harm you, and you need protection to survive. You can either disarm the dangerous pointed object, or arm yourself for protection.

Look out the windows of your living or working space. Are there any points aimed in your direction ("secret arrows of Qi"), that you have not seen before? The closer and larger the "point" the more adverse the affect will be. The idea is to disarm the harmful Qi aimed your way. You can hang a pointed object or mirror above the doorway. You can block the view with an object. Or, a large wind sock, whirlygig, or moving weather vane can be placed in the pathway to divert the Qi flow.

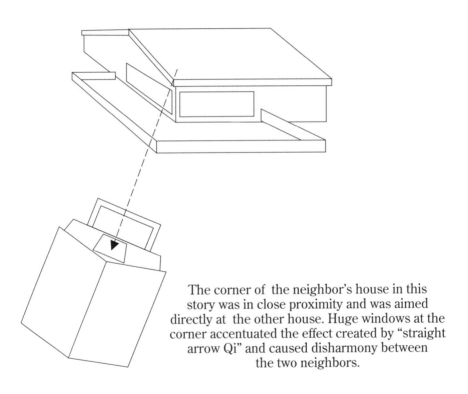

The corner of the neighbor's house in this story was in close proximity and was aimed directly at the other house. Huge windows at the corner accentuated the effect created by "straight arrow Qi" and caused disharmony between the two neighbors.

To Buy or Not to Buy

A 35-year-old woman held a good position in a computer software company. She was chief of the marketing department and earned a substantial salary. After a couple of years, she had saved enough money for a downpayment on a house. She found a house that she liked on hillside with a gorgeous view of the Pacific Ocean. She had heard a lot about Feng Shui from a friend, and felt it was important to have a consultation before buying this house.

We met the realtor there on a beautiful, sunny day. The house had a large, attractive front yard. The Feng Shui was good because it was level and there was a lot of greenery.

The realtor seemed a little confused by the conversation between her excited client and a strange Chinese man! She fumbled with the key to open the front door. The family room had sliding glass doors with an expansive ocean view. Whitecaps peeked out from the deep blue, and the waves broke on the shore below. We stepped outside onto the deck and I discovered that although the house had a big front yard, its back yard was almost nonexistent. The back of the house was extremely close to a steep, towering hillside.

After touring the rest of the house, I asked the real estate agent how many years the previous owners lived there, and why they decided to sell. She said they had stayed two years, and left when their business went bankrupt. The couple then divorced, and put the house on the market. Even though the house had some redeeming features, there were some definite negative qualities to consider. In the end, I recommended my client not buy the house, and explained my reasons to her.

Summary

Usually, a house built too close to an extremely steep hillside is not good Feng Shui. This precarious placement could bring about feelings of instability. In this story, the hill was so close that if anything were to fall down the hill, including bad Qi, it would literally drop right on top of the house.

Ideally, the front of the house should be somewhat lower than the back, facing a good view. There should be a slightly elevated backyard with a hill a little distance away. The hill would serve as natural protection from the elements, and a support or "spine" for the site.

On a more practical note, multi-million dollar homes built on steep hillsides often incur damage from excessive rainfall and mud slides. During a storm you may not sleep as soundly as usual—how much more troubled the sleep of someone fearing a mud slide must be!

When buying a house, find out why the previous owners decided to move. If they were doing better financially and wanted to upgrade to a nicer home, this is a positive sign, you will inherit the good Qi from the past. If the previous owners were doing poorly and could not afford to keep the home, then stop and consider; you could inherit negative Qi from past failures.

The decision to buy a house or business property should not depend solely on the previous owners' reasons for selling. But if in addition to a negative reason for the previous owners' move, the Feng Shui is very difficult to correct, then it may not be the best purchase.

However, if the Feng Shui is correctable, you can alter the residual negative elements from past failures. This can be done in part by cleaning, painting, and redecorating. A reputable Feng Shui master can perform special ceremonies to completely clear negative Qi. You can also perform your own special prayer or ceremony, whatever you feel comfortable with, to bring uplifting Qi.

Martini or Cognac?

An old friend of mine from Taiwan owned a Chinese restaurant in Arizona, and through the years had prospered in business. Eventually, he built a nice home on a 7½ acre lot, strewn with native giant saguaro cactus and boulders. The property was rustic and beautiful, and he decided to leave it in its natural state.

Three or four years after that, he noticed his savings had not increased as in the past. After assessing his finances, he realized that although he was still turning over about the same cash flow, he was unable to save money. Being very practical, he realized there must be a reason for this discrepancy. Being raised Taiwanese, he was familiar with Feng Shui, and contacted me for a reading. It just so happened I was scheduled in three weeks for a business meeting in Phoenix. I would be able to drop by afterward.

We met first at his restaurant, and I found there was nothing overtly wrong with the Feng Shui there. In fact, he applied what he knew about it before he opened the restaurant. I only made a few suggestions. My friend, as thorough as usual, wrote everything down in a small notebook which he carried everywhere with him.

He had arranged for an elaborate Chinese meal for lunch; and because the food and company were so engaging, we arrived at his home past dusk.

My friend's home had a pleasant, warm atmosphere. I checked the directional Feng Shui with my loupan (instrument to determine proper direction in Feng Shui), then investigated the rest of the house. Again, I found most everything in good order, and suggested only a few small changes. I told him I would have liked to see the grounds in daylight, because it was an extremely important part of the reading. He immediately insisted that I be his guest for the night. Besides, he reasoned, it was far too late to travel.

It was already warm the next morning when we stepped outside. I walked the property's circumference, noticing how pleasant it was. But as I approached the main gate, a Feng Shui error was instantly obvious. His property was not square, but oddly shaped. The driveway was at the side that was much wider than the opposite end. My friend wanted to understand, so I borrowed his notebook and sketched an analogy for him.

I explained because the entrance was on the widest side of the lot, it caused an energetic situation where things can easily be in his possession, but

Expensive cognac is served in the left glass, so one precious drop will not spill. A cheap martini is served in the right glass, which is easy to spill, even if it is only your first! The plot had the same shape as the martini glass. Adding bushes to the sides of the plot made it more like a cognac glass.

because of the wide opening, things also left quickly. Therefore, it became difficult for him to hold onto profits.

He was concerned because rerouting his driveway would be a costly project. I said there was an easier solution: plant a waist-high border of bushes near the entry. This would make the the entrance appear smaller than it actually was. Because the row of bushes wouldn't cover the entire area, I also suggested planting a rose garden on the other side of the bushes.

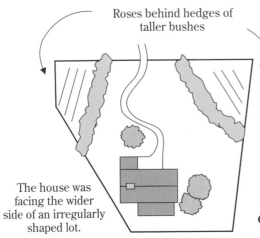

Roses behind hedges of taller bushes

The house was facing the wider side of an irregularly shaped lot.

Since that Feng Shui reading, the restaurant is doing well, he made a deposit into his savings account, and his wife enjoys the roses.

Summary

The plot of land a house is sitting on is the Qi foundation. The shape, levelness, terrain, and foliage should all be considered. In general, square, rectangular, or circular lots are the best—in other words, a balanced form.

A level plot is most preferred, even if it is on a mountainside. On a level lot the house should be positioned in the center or a little into the back section. If you happen to have a sloped plot, the home should be positioned on the higher side faced toward the lower side.

This story offered a creative solution to a difficult plot of land. Another cure may be a spotlight strategically placed to give the visual appearance that an area is smoother, more level, or of a different shape.

The Dead Water Pond

Not long ago, a friend of mine bought a house in the Los Angeles area. The previous owner had built a pond in the front of the house near the driveway, close to the main entrance. Because the house was on the market for a while before she moved in, it was left uninhabited, and the pond was left unkept. It became dried and dirty, and the pump, through disuse, no longer worked. Because of the damage, it would require some work and expense to make repairs.

When my friend bought the house, she wanted to keep the little pond, because she heard that it was good Feng Shui. She cleaned it up, bought fish, made it pretty, and was quite pleased with it.

She had lived in the house for about a year when her health began to fail. She gained weight and began to feel fatigued and depressed. She felt progressively weaker and fell ill quite often.

When visiting relatives in Los Angeles, I stopped by her house. She had called me in San Diego seeking advice about her health, and I suspected that her living environment was affecting her. When I called to say I could do a Feng Shui reading, she promised to have delicious tea waiting.

I parked my car on the street and walked up the driveway to her house. I stopped and watched the fish. They were active and appeared healthy, even though the water was cloudy and dirty.

My hostess did prepare a nice snack, over which we discussed her house and the little pond. I asked her where the water was being supplied from and about drainage. Because the fish seemed to be healthy, she decided to save money and did not replace the broken pump. The water was not continually replaced, but she would occasionally dump a fresh bucket of water into the pond.

I recommended that if she wanted to keep the pond, the water must be fresh and circulated to prevent it from becoming stagnant. She should have a pump system with a filter to keep the water clean. If proper care of the pond proved to be a financial burden or too time consuming, it would be better to fill the pond with soil and make it into a flower bed. I explained that although a fish pond is good Feng Shui, it creates the adverse effect if it is stagnant and dirty.

My friend decided to keep the fish pond and completely clean it up. Six months later her health began to improve, and she felt much happier, not as depressed as before. She also found a more satisfying job that opened a new career possibility for her.

Summary

Water is symbolic of prosperity and brings good luck. A properly placed pond or pool can be a very powerful enhancement. Many famous structures are built with pools of water, such as the Taj Mahal in India, and the Washington Monument mall area.

There are some important things to keep in mind about pools or ponds—their influence can be very powerful, whether positive or negative. The body of water should be in proportion to the dwelling. If there is too much water it will cause a "drowning" effect. The pool should not be too close to the dwelling; the Yin influence of water may be too strong, causing excessive "dampness" conditions. In Chinese Medicine the term "dampness" as applied to health refers to urinary problems, upper respiratory congestion, or weight gain.

The Chinese term for stagnant or dirty water is "dead water." This expression is not only literal, but also means that your luck will be "stuck or stagnant." It is quite possible that someone living in a house with a stagnant pond (or swimming pool) will incur respiratory problems, misfortune, or weight gain as the person in this story did.

Prescription for Success

A long-time friend of mine, a forty-year-old pharmacist, worked in Queens, New York. After many years of saving money, he decided to invest it. However, over three years time, the various investments he chose all lost money. Despite excellent financial advice and careful choices, his bad track record prompted him to wonder if Feng Shui could turn his situation around.

While stopping in New York City on my way overseas, we met for lunch and he asked me to do a Feng Shui reading for his home. We drove there, and as we pulled into his driveway, I saw there was a huge dead tree in his front yard. It was close to the front door and in direct alignment with it. He said the tree had been dead quite a while, and stood there for years. He hadn't removed it right away because it would have been a difficult and expensive procedure. He was so busy working at the pharmacy and with his investments that he had all but forgotten about removing the dead tree. I suggested he spend a couple hundred dollars and immediately remove it. The ground should be leveled to blend in with the rest of the lawn. He could also use the wood from the tree in his fireplace.

I returned home, and we lost touch for a while. Three years after the Feng Shui consultation, he visited me in California on his way to Asia on business. His investments had been quite profitable since he saw me, and he was venturing into new business. He was excited by this particular trip because he was going to Singapore to establish a company that would import and export pharmaceuticals, and he knew it was going to be a success.

Summary

One important rule of Feng Shui is to never have a large tree growing directly in front of the main entrance to the house. It is especially bad if the tree is dead. This situation is thought to bring misfortune to the residents, particularly for their financial situation. Of course, trees usually represent the good Qi of growth and life. But, if the tree grows very large and obscures the doorway, then it can draw energy away from the house—in the same way a large tree can deplete the soil surrounding it. Often, the soil is so poor that grass cannot even grow underneath. A very large tree could also have that kind of effect energetically, sapping the vital energy away from the house it dominates. As a rule of thumb, the land directly in front of a main entrance should be clear and open: a level, flat space so that good Qi can flow in unobstructed. Grading the surrounding land, or constructing a deck or patio over an uneven area, can create that kind of space.

Trees can be used to enhance or protect a house. Trees or shrubs placed on either side of a doorway or driveway can serve to temper invading Qi. A tree can be strategically placed between an unhealthy neighbor or harsh street traffic to ward off their ill effects.

Changing Minds About Vines

A successful architect decided to purchase a piece of commercial property in the beach area. He designed plans for it with three buildings that would complement one another's unique design. Although he was schooled in the United States, he was also open-minded about different cultures. Because he had several Chinese clients in the past, he was familiar with Feng Shui, and was intrigued by the possibility of employing it in his own designs. Because the property and buildings involved a substantial investment of his own money, he sought advice on Feng Shui. He called one of his previous Chinese clients for a reference, and they gave him my name.

We met over coffee at his office. He spread the blueprints over several tables. He proceeded to show me the layout of the buildings, doors, internal layout, and even landscaping. I gave suggestions to correct Feng Shui here and there, taking time to briefly explain my reasoning. He altered the plans accordingly before construction began.

After the major construction work was complete, he called me for another session for the decoration and color. We planned a site visit for this stage in the process.

I was impressed by my client's creativity in designing this project. The buildings had beautiful horizontal and vertical lines created by wood planks across the front of each that complemented the surroundings. This simple effect created a harmonious and attractive architectural language. He gushed with deserved pride when I complimented him, hitched his thumb in his Levis, and began to describe his landscaping plans. He wanted the grounds planted with a number of vine-type plants that would climb and intertwine with the wood planks. He envisioned the building facades covered with vines to give them character.

At this point I strongly advised against this part of the landscaping. He hesitated, but I continued to press the issue. I told him that overgrown vines were not necessarily good Feng Shui for business offices. I jokingly challenged him to go ahead with his plans to have vines crawl everywhere, and just see if he wouldn't start having business or legal trouble! I also reminded him that the effect of the wooden planks would be lost if covered over by vines. My client laughed wholeheartedly, conceded to my suggestion, and planted the grounds with varieties of unusual decorative trees.

Summary

When considering the use of vine-type plants for decoration, it is important to keep some things in mind: the vines should not block out natural light; there is adequate air flow from windows, doorways, and walkways; the vines are trimmed back close and have a neat appearance, not overgrown and shabby.

If vines are dense, old, and overgrown, they create a depressing energy that instills feelings of constriction (see the story "Plant Takeover," page 218). Overgrown vines create energy best described by a scene in an old science fiction movie classic I saw years ago. The movie featured alien plants intent on conquering mankind. They sprouted from the ground, their vines like fingers, and reached up to pull their next unwary victim to death underground.

The Qi created by overgrown vines may create problems in professions involving investigation and litigation, or any activities that entangle the "victim."

The Hyperactive Clinic

An alternative health care clinic was open about five months when trouble started. Classic signs of anxiety began to show in the personnel, which ultimately affected their job performance. Judging from their past job history, the personnel manager regarded all the staff to be high-caliber. He couldn't pinpoint clear reasons for their stress, even after talking personally with some of them. The director knew a little about Feng Shui, so after consulting with the entire staff, asked me to give a Feng Shui reading.

As I turned the corner that would bring me to the street the clinic was on, I realized that I was driving straight toward the clinic building. The street dead-ended directly in line with it at a 'T' intersection. The clinic was on the first floor, at street level. As I pulled into the parking lot, I noticed that the entrance was a double-wide glass door. I understood the whole situation without stepping foot into the clinic. Only after touring the facility, and offering a few suggestions to correct interior Feng Shui, did I explain the major problem.

The clinic was at the junction of an extremely busy 'T' shaped intersection. Traffic was bottle-necked here because of a traffic signal, and the entire day cars were turning every direction (see illustration page 147). This frenetic activity was taking place directly in front of the clinic's wide double glass doors. Anyone exposed to this from the entrance/reception area for a period of time would understandably be affected. Some car's brakes might suddenly fail and the car would crash right into the clinic!

I suggested they build a wall directly in front of the clinic entrance. It need not be very high, maybe only three or four feet. This would give a sense of security and block the disturbing street traffic energy. I strongly recommended in the near future moving the entrance to the side of the building near the parking lot.

The director decided to construct the wall. A few months later, he had the entrance moved. The employees were much more relaxed because their work environment improved tremendously.

Summary

Psychologically, the mind "tends to believe what it sees, more than by reason." People naturally become nervous when they are exposed to a dangerous-appearing view. A car speeding out of control could easily smash through glass doors, but when the view is blocked it provides peace of mind.

In Feng Shui, any building at the juncture of a T-shaped intersection is affected by adverse Qi from the street traffic activity. The building becomes the target of harsh, penetrating, and invasive Qi. Today, we travel much faster than ever before. The ill effects of such Qi movement is magnified beyond any level our ancestors were ever exposed to. It is more important than ever to be aware of Feng Shui in our fast-paced, stress-filled world.

The best solution was to move the clinic
doors away from the street to the side
of the building facing the parking lot

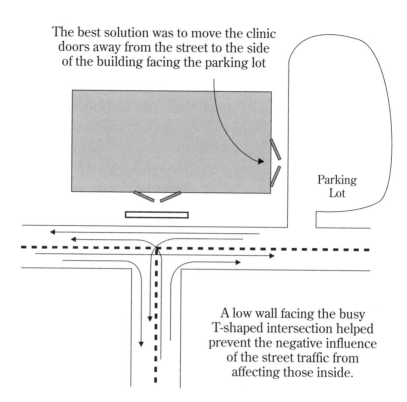

Parking
Lot

A low wall facing the busy
T-shaped intersection helped
prevent the negative influence
of the street traffic from
affecting those inside.

In and Out of the Curve

About four years ago, I treated a man for shoulder pain sustained from a car accident. He was very interested in Chinese culture and thought, and was always reading a variety of related topics. He had discovered a book about Chinese astrology, and after going through it, realized that the previous year had been quite unlucky for him. A number of unfortunate occurrences had taken place, and he suspected that it wasn't mere coincidence.

The previous year he had the car accident and missed work for a period of time. He was ill far more often. Usually he only caught one small cold every other year or so. He also suffered a substantial financial loss because of a dishonest businessman he met at that time.

Because I was Chinese, he was very interested in my opinion about Chinese astrology and fortune telling with the Ba Gwa and I-Ching. I told him I was not an expert in astrology and fortune telling, but that I used the Ba Gwa and I-Ching in Feng Shui. He kept this information in the back of his mind.

With acupuncture, in a little over two months he was pain-free and strong again. As we concluded the final treatment, he invited me to his house for a Feng Shui reading.

The couple had been living in their present home for only two years. From his directions I knew their house was in a middle- to upper-class neighborhood. He told me the house had a view, and I took in the seascape as I pulled my car into the driveway. I felt an ocean breeze and breathed in the scent of night-blooming jasmine as I rang their doorbell.

They both answered and immediately offered me something to drink. We chatted about the ancient history of Feng Shui as we walked through the house. I had known from the minute I pulled into the driveway what the main Feng Shui error was, but completed the reading for the interior before I addressed it. At last, I set down my cup of tea and sketched an example in my notebook. Their house was built on the convex side of a sharp curved section of the winding street. It was on a hillside facing the ocean, about 50 feet below street level. Their driveway was steep and straight down.

I tactfully told them that their house was not situated in the best location. Not only were they on the outside of a curve, but they were far below the level of the street. If a car were to lose control at the curve, it would plunge down their driveway and run into the front door. They were in a precarious position—like sitting ducks.

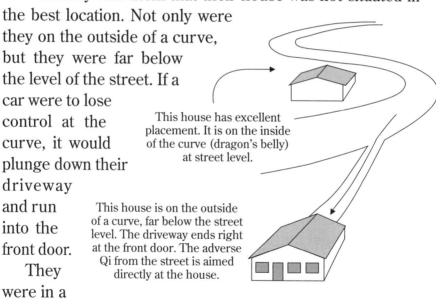

This house has excellent placement. It is on the inside of the curve (dragon's belly) at street level.

This house is on the outside of a curve, far below the street level. The driveway ends right at the front door. The adverse Qi from the street is aimed directly at the house.

The best solution was to sell the house and move. But, that was out of the question for them since they recently bought the house. Of course they could correct the Feng

Shui, but it would take a little work. A barrier needed to be placed between the house and street, such as a strong wall, or a thick line of trees to deflect the adverse Qi.

Their steep driveway was located right at the most angled part of the curved road. Qi flows much like water, and the adverse Qi from the street activity went right down their driveway. Pillars, or large trees on either side of the driveway entrance would help block that flow. Placing a moving object there, such as a whirlygig, would also help deter the effects of negative Qi.

Summary

This kind of precarious and vulnerable placement on the "outside of a curve" is traditionally considered bad luck to the Chinese. It was thought to be linked with accidents, illness, and sudden tragedy. In keeping with modern thought, Feng Shui should be based on practical reality—misfortunes should not be credited to mysterious forces. Logically, a house on the outside of a curve would cause unconscious feelings of uneasiness because of its precarious placement. Whatever accident or "bad luck" that befell residents could have a myriad of causes, but nervous distraction could impair one's peace of mind, health—and judgment.

Neighbors, Fighting Doors

About six years ago, a good friend and colleague, whom I shall call John, came to my office after hours. We wanted to go over specs on a piece of equipment we were both thinking about buying. Afterwards, we chatted a while. He was happy with his work, but was irritated by the next door neighbor at home. I pressed him to share the details.

About a year ago, John rented a house in a newer subdivision of San Diego. He never had a vegetable garden before, and decided to plant a small plot in the backyard. He got carried away when he planted the front with rose bushes, but was thrilled when they produced an abundance of colorful blooms.

The problems started soon after he moved in. The neighbor didn't introduce himself, or offer a friendly handshake when their paths crossed for the first time. Instead, he gave an offhanded insult, saying John was not conforming with the landscaping standards by covering the front yard with scraggly bushes. John was taken aback by this direct affront, but being good-natured, easily dismissed the neighbor's rudeness. Later on, the neighbor left a note on his door threatening to report him to the housing commission, adding they "didn't need his kind here." Once after tending his roses, John inadvertently left a garden tool outside. Unaware he was being watched, the nasty neighbor walked into John's yard and promptly tossed the tool into a garbage can. The neighbor continually did insulting and destructive things.

During the course of our conversation, John invited my

family over for dinner. I accepted, and told him I could do a Feng Shui reading while we were there. When we arrived, my wife admired John's roses. At the same time, I noticed that the offending neighbor's front door was directly facing John's front door. They were in relatively close proximity, with nothing to break the view. As John offered us hors d'oeuvres, we stepped out to the front yard, and I explained that the alignment of the two doors was bad Feng Shui. He listened thoughtfully as he mused over the situation.

I then offered a cure to reduce the opposing energy created by the two doors. I said to get a sharply pointed object from a hardware store, or construct something with that shape, and place it so it pointed at the neighbor's front door. I also told him to hang a Ba Gwa mirror above his front door. These two objects would deflect the neighbor's negative energy, and serve as a protective force for his home.

Two months later, John mentioned the neighbor basically kept to himself, and had stopped harassing him. Eventually, John built a fence that blocked their views of each other, which was even more effective in relieving the neighborly tensions. They even did a couple of small favors for one another. Then the once-hostile neighbor surprised John with a Christmas fruit basket that year.

Summary

For a house, condo, apartment, or place of business, pay special attention to the placement and proximity of the doors in relation to neighbors' doors. It is especially problematic if doors are close and in direct alignment. The Chinese term for this situation, "fighting doors," explains what may happen to residents with doors aligned this way. Of course, the best solution is not to live in a house with opposing doors. But there are some things to do other than move. The front door could be relocated; or, the view between "fighting doors" could be blocked by a tree, wall, or fountain; or, other inexpensive Feng Shui cures could be employed.

A "fighting doors" situation could also exist inside. Opposing office doors may affect employee morale and cooperation. Bedroom "fighting doors" could possibly cause sibling rivalry. A small hallway that has many doors could also cause conflict because of the overabundance of activity. A bright hall light, soothing color, and placement of a Feng Shui tool such as a crystal, will help offset the situation.

Mouth of the House

A middle-aged couple had been sick constantly since contracting the flu six months ago. They had lingering upper respiratory symptoms; their flu just never went away. After a month of treatment with acupuncture, an herbal formula, and diet, their symptoms weren't resolved. Their upper respiratory tracts were still not clear, and the wife began to wheeze at night. Before referring them out to a Western medical specialist, I decided to talk to them about Feng Shui. They agreed that it might help explain their prolonged illness and scheduled a reading.

Their house, built in the 1930s, had been beautifully remodeled. A 10° drop in temperature was evident when I stepped into the front door, even though it was a warm day. I suggested opening the window shades on sunny days to allow in fresh air, natural light, and warmth. They could also occasionally use the fireplace for warmth in the evenings.

When I went back outside to check the front of the house, the side yard drew my attention, where I saw a big trash can. There was no door nearby to empty the kitchen trash from the back. The only way they could empty it was to take it out the front door, and then around to the gate which led to the side yard. This "backward movement" of trash was probably the bad Feng Shui that was affecting them.

It is bad Feng Shui to take trash out from the front door, but it is even worse to bring it close to the house again by keeping it in the side yard. Ideally, trash should be taken out from the back or side of the house straight to the sidewalk.

They unwittingly kept bringing trash back into their environment—consequently, their illnesses kept returning!

The solution was to either add a sliding glass door from the kitchen so they could access the garbage area without going through the entire house, or knock out a five-foot wall that blocked access to the side yard from the back yard. Then they could go through the back door directly to the side and dump the trash.

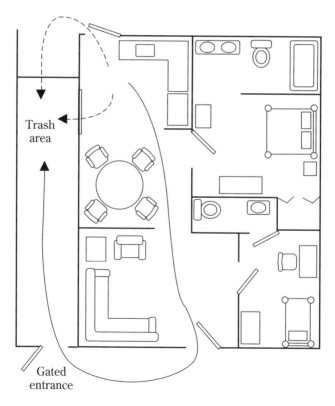

Before, trash was taken out the front door to the side of the house as shown by the solid line. As shown by the broken lines, the correction was either to remove the wall so they could use the kitchen door, or install a door in the dining room to gain access to the trash area.

They were surprised when I asked them how they got along with their in-laws. The husband replied it was amicable, although they often argued and were hard to please. Lately, the relationship with his in-laws was especially strained. I explained that their trash cans were located in the "relatives" position of the house (see Chapter 5 for locations). If they knocked out the five-foot wall the "relatives" position would not be so adversely affected. Their health, and the relationship with their relatives, could benefit by this change. This convinced them to remove the wall.

They haven't had any lingering respiratory infections three years following the corrected Feng Shui. If one of them became sick, usually one or two acupuncture treatments or taking herbs for a couple days would clear it up. Although I never asked about their in-laws, they didn't complain about them either!

Summary

Obviously, a drafty house was bad for this couple's health and would exacerbate a lingering illness. But, there was more going on for them here.

It is equally as important to be aware of how Qi flows into the house, as to how it flows out. In Feng Shui, the front entrance of a house or building is considered the "mouth of the house." In this case, trash was being spit out the mouth, then swallowed back up again! The flow of Qi was unhealthy.

Often, there is more than one thing in an environment that causes bad Feng Shui, and it takes a little detective work, and sometimes carefully asked questions, to uncover every problem.

Data Operator's Dead End

A young woman who worked as an input operator for a data management firm was having difficulty with her job. She also experienced some depression in her personal life. A friend who owned a bookstore that became more profitable after a Feng Shui reading suggested she contact me for advice.

She confided in me instantly over the phone. She was depressed about almost every aspect of her life, including work and family. She felt irritable and restless much of the time, and new situations made her fearful. She was also frustrated because she was with the same firm five years, and had not received any of the promotions she applied for, nor had she received a significant raise during her time there.

As we discussed her situation, I sensed she definitely had an energetic block holding her down. She was delighted to have a Feng Shui reading done for her apartment.

I discovered that the entrance to her apartment was at the end of a very long, dark, and narrow hallway. This kind of hallway is just like a dead-end street. It is generally not good Feng Shui to be placed on an energetic dead-end. Every time she walked down the hallway, she ended up at her doorway: the dead-end of the Qi flow. A person living behind such a door may experience frustration in business or in their personal life. They may feel held back—unable to receive promotions, or miss opportunities. Eventually, this "Qi stagnation" would make a person feel hopeless about the future. The young data entry operator recognized that those kinds of feelings started surfacing after moving into this apartment.

I told her she didn't necessarily have to move; she liked the place and the view from her balcony. I suggested she hang a mirror on the outside of the doorway to her apartment. The mirror in this case is not only used to deflect negative Qi, but to reflect the open end of the hallway. As she walked toward the door she would be able to see what was behind her, instead of just the hallway dead-end. I specified that the mirror should be large enough so that she had a good view of what was behind and around her; in this way the dead-end image would be dispelled.

After putting up a mirror as I instructed, she slowly began to feel an emotional weight was being lifted. She was a much happier person, and after four months, she was promoted to a management position.

Summary

It should be noted that a Feng Shui cure does not impart a mysterious power, or instantly bring us wealth or position. It is usually just good common sense. Most likely, the client's mind was comforted by the view from the mirror. It made her feel less confined, as well as safer because she could see what was around her, and consequently, happier. The promotion was probably deserved because her superiors noticed her improved attitude.

A house at the end of a dead-end street may also suffer the effects from Qi stagnation, and may become the "target object" for adverse Qi funneled in by the street. Several things can be done. The idea is to block, deflect, or move Qi along. Large trees, fences, or pillars along the driveway would block the Qi. A whirlygig, large flag, fountain, or other moving object will keep Qi moving. A floodlight or mirror will deflect Qi. And of course, the ideal is not to live at a dead-end.

Fresher Seafood Restaurant

A few years ago, a new seafood restaurant in Southern California was not as busy as it should have been. The restaurant was located on a hillside with a panoramic, seascape view. The owner designed the plans himself, and couldn't understand why business hadn't picked up. He had attended to every detail: food, design, service, and location. He hired a creative chef, whose dishes were delicious works of art. By his estimation, it should have been swamped with patrons.

The restaurant owner had a friend who had attended one of my Feng Shui seminars, and she encouraged him to ask my advice about the place.

Immediately upon entering the restaurant I saw a convex, half-moon shaped bar. The owner thought a large, impressive bar at the entry would accommodate waiting diners during busy dinner hours. Typically, Western-style bars are dimly lit, as this one was, and the wood was a dark-stained mahogany. A few tables could be seen immediately upon entering which spilled over from the main dining room. There was also a 2' wide x 3' high x 15' long divider between the bar and main dining area. The plants on the divider were doing poorly in the dim light. They were yellowing and covered with thick dust and spider webs.

As I walked around, I began suggesting a few changes, trying to inspire the owner about the kind of atmosphere that could be created. I suggested a completely different shape for the bar: concave, and that it be lengthened. The tables should be moved back into the main dining room. I also suggested installing more lighting in the bar and hanging a bright, colorful painting above a sofa near the doorway with spotlights trained on it. The door should be relocated to open into the center of the reception/bar area, instead of the far left corner. The divider needed a fresh change too, so I proposed placing a large, lighted aquarium there, stocked with brightly colored fish.

I also made a practical suggestion regarding the waiter's station: Move it to another location so the service could flow more smoothly. I had been a waiter in my youth, which gave me insight into how to make the service more efficient.

The owner made the changes, and also installed a huge, brilliant chandelier at the entry. The bar and door were re-built, and the walls were painted with cool, bright colors. The divider was replaced by a long, beautiful aquarium.

The first month after the changes were made, business increased by 50 percent. After four months, the restaurant had an increase from the previous year's profits of 250 percent! Now, years later, it is the most popular restaurant in the area.

Summary

This restaurant had just about everything going for it. But it was hard for diners to get past the dark entrance to discover it all! The shape of the bar (see before illustration) actually "pushed" customers out the door. A rounded shape is not necessarily offensive in Feng Shui. But, a round, protruding (convex) shape would not necessarily draw customers inside either. In this case, the bar was so dark and in such close proximity to the door, that the overall effect it created was repelling to customers. It made them feel as if they should only have a quick drink and leave. A concave shape was preferable for the bar, an inviting form that prompted customers to come in and fill up the space. Bright, colorful decor with plenty of light created an inviting reception.

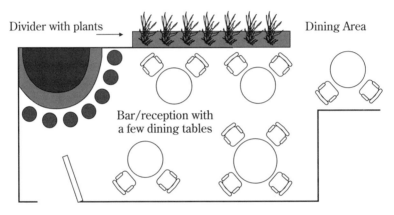

Before, the restaurant had a congested, less-welcome atmosphere: a dark, convex-shaped bar; dusty plants; crowded tables and poor lighting.

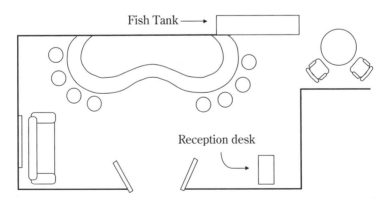

After, patrons were greeted with a friendlier decor: a bright entry with a couch and colorful paintings. The bar was changed to a concave shape with light colored wood, and the entry opened into the center of the room.

Banker Who Couldn't Save

A bank vice-president had been working in his present position for over 12 years, with an extremely good salary. He had a large home, around 3,500 square feet, in a fairly upscale neighborhood. But even though his salary was quite in excess of his living expenses, he found it difficult to save money. In addition, he'd become progressively more lethargic and fatigued. His first impulse when he came home from work was to immediately head for his bedroom upstairs and take a nap. He felt as if he were rapidly aging.

I was referred to the banker by his masseur, who thought I might be able to help him. I had suggested a Feng Shui solution to the masseur over the telephone, and the banker asked if I could do the same for him. I told him I would have to do a reading at his house, because this was a more complicated case. We agreed on an appointment.

As I pulled my car in front of his house, I could see he had a scenic canyon view. The front yard was attractive and well manicured. The banker swung the door wide open when I rang the bell. A stairway directly in front of me leading to the second floor immediately caught my attention. It was about three feet wide and dimly lit. There was a conspicuous air-conditioning duct on the stairway ceiling. It looked like you could possibly hit your head on it going up or down the stairs.

I explained the detrimental effects of the stairway and gave a number of options to correct the Feng Shui. First, change the location of the stairway so that it could be

163

accessed from a different direction. This would remove the view of it from the main entrance. Second, remove the air-conditioning duct to increase the height of the stairway ceiling. I also suggested installing a skylight over the stairs. And finally, if the stairway were to be relocated, he should widen it to be more in proportion with the size of his home.

At first the banker was hesitant to spend any money on this project. But he quickly decided it was worth investing in something that could improve his health and mental outlook, especially since he was recently diagnosed with borderline chronic fatigue syndrome. After weighing the benefits against the costs, he decided to remodel.

He then undertook the project wholeheartedly. He had the stairway moved, installed a skylight, and rerouted the air-conditioning duct. He also had the stairway widened to four-and-a-half feet.

Once the remodeling was completed, the banker's physical and mental health began to show steady improvement. His energy slowly returned, and he no longer needed afternoon naps. A year and a half later, I heard the banker had saved enough money to purchase property with a four-unit rental.

Summary

It is extremely undesirable to have the entrance of a stairway directly in line with the main entrance. Many Chinese people would not even live in such a house. Stairways, whether descending, ascending, or spiral, draw Qi away. Stairways placed in close proximity to the main entrance would cause the beneficial "welcoming Qi" to be sucked away. This would eventually cause residents to feel fatigued or experience financial drain. Also, stairways should not be directly in the center of the house. The center of your house represents the center of the body—the digestive system. A stairway here may eventually lead to digestive problems.

Because the stairway was the first thing our bank vice-president saw when he came home from work, his first impulse was to go upstairs and take a nap. The narrowness and darkness of his stairway accentuated the negative drain, making the banker fatigued and lethargic. The stairway just "sucked" him right up to his bed!

The bad Feng Shui created by the stairway was extreme in this story, so drastic changes were needed. But moving a stairway is a sizable expense, and there are other remedies that can correct the Feng Shui. A large, healthy plant could be placed at the foot of the stairway. The plant would impart upward-moving, positive life-energy in the same direction as the stairway, lessening the stairway's negative influence. Or a wind chime can be placed between the stairway and the main entrance to disperse the Qi flow. The welcoming Qi would not be immediately drawn away. If the ceiling above the stairway is low, as in this story, a mirror can be placed on the stairway ceiling or wall to create a visually larger space. Another helpful solution would be to install a light in the stairway—a simple Feng Shui cure to bring positive Qi.

Qi Superhighway

A Chinese family of four, relatively new to the United States, decided to make their home in Monterey Park, a section of Los Angeles. They had carefully planned the move and thought it was a good decision for the whole family. However, within a six-month period, they experienced several unfortunate events which dampened their excitement about their move.

Being Chinese, they were raised with some understanding of Feng Shui, and looked for problems with their home. But eventually they decided to have a professional reading. It seemed beyond coincidence that so many unfortunate things happened in such a short time. They were referred to me by a mutual friend, and I scheduled time for them during an upcoming trip to visit relatives in Los Angeles.

Their house was on a square, level lot, with a nice view of the city. The surrounding environment was pleasant, with good Qi flow. Inside, every room had plenty of natural light. The house had a good basic layout for adequate air flow and Qi circulation. From this brief overview, I thought the house had good Feng Shui. But when I walked to the back bedroom, I realized it had one long, straight hallway from the front door to the back of the house, where there was a large picture window.

Hallways that cut from the front to the back of the house in one straight line create what is termed in Chinese as "straight arrow Qi." This straight path causes Qi to accelerate, making it behave like a fast river, sweeping everything away with it. This leaves an energetic void, and unfortunately, the inhabitants of this house were suffering the detriment in their personal and financial pursuits. They felt they had become victims to the whims of bad luck.

I gave my clients an inexpensive solution. I told them to hang strung beads across the hallway just after the first set of doors. This would soften the Qi flow by creating a partial barrier. The sound of the beads when they walked through would accentuate their dispersing action. They asked me what could be done temporarily while they searched stores for the decorative beads. I told them to hang a wind chime in the location where the beads were to be strung.

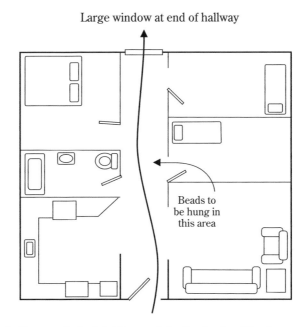

The long hallway cut straight through to the back of the house. Beads, wind chimes, or a decorative banner would help slow and soften the Qi flow.

Summary

The "straight arrow Qi" in their hallway created a Qi superhighway—the Qi sped straight through the house, then left. The bad Feng Shui of a long, straight hallway is magnified if there is a large window at the opposite end, even worse if it is a door. The house would literally be cut in half, eventually causing digestive trouble, financial stress, or strife among those in the household. (A house divided in half may cause residents to be divided against each other!)

Good Qi should fill a house, making it a reservoir to nourish and sustain its inhabitants. Pathways through the house should allow Qi to slowly meander back and forth. That is why many pathways in China are not built straight, but are graceful and winding.

Wall That Blocked All

Bill and Jesse asked me to do a Feng Shui reading of their house because of recent personal and business difficulties. On entering their new home, I was impressed by the beautiful entryway, hanging chandelier, and oval Persian rugs. The opulent interior design was sophisticated and tasteful. I continued to walk through their home, but kept returning to the front entryway. There did not seem to be a warm and welcoming atmosphere.

While standing there, I reflected back to the story Bill initially told me:

"When our arguments caused Jesse to move out of our bedroom and into the guest room, I became very worried. Until now we never experienced this much aggravation in our relationship of twenty years. We also took a loss at the store this month, which only added to the tension.

"After living in Hong Kong last year, I became a firm believer in Feng Shui. A couple of weeks ago I realized that the riff between Jesse and me started not long after we moved in. When our furniture store had its only loss in eight years last month, I knew something was wrong. It dawned on me that we had not considered the Feng Shui of this house, and it might be affecting us."

The layout of the house, and what Bill and Jesse told me, confirmed for me that the Feng Shui at the front entryway was the main problem. An entryway should be constructed to allow the good environmental Qi to flow into the house. Their welcoming Qi was hindered by a wall that was too close to the front doorway. It blocked virtually all the good Qi and repelled it back out. This "Qi deprivation" eventually caused havoc in their finances and personal life.

To correct the Feng Shui, the wall needed to be moved back about seven feet from its present position. It was not a weight-bearing wall, so they decided to move it back as I suggested.

Within two weeks after the construction was completed, business picked up. After a four-week period, the conflicting personal emotions leveled off for the couple, and they felt as solid and content as before in their relationship.

Summary

A home is meant to be an energy reservoir from which the occupants can draw. Good environmental Qi should flow into the house from the entry that is used most. There are a few ways to correct the Feng Shui besides moving a wall. An extended entryway can be built to provide depth and expansiveness, and will allow for Qi to flow into the house. An entryway or foyer that is too narrow will also hinder flow of good Qi—a mirror could be hung on a foyer wall to visually expand the space. If a door opens in such a way that it makes a cramped or clumsy entrance, the Qi flow will also be obstructed. A better entrance may be achieved by rehanging the door to open on the other side.

An entry can also be too large. The Qi flow can be overwhelming and the residents may feel overwhelmed right along with it. The idea is to have an entrance that is in proportion to the size of the structure.

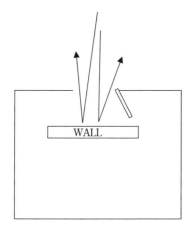 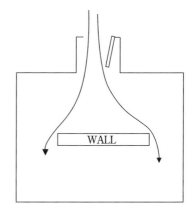

A wall too close to the entry deflects incoming Qi and does not allow the natural, gentle flow to enter the home and nourish the residents.

Moving the wall back allows good Qi to enter the house. Or, an extended entryway will funnel Qi inward so it will not be repelled by the wall.

Screening Out Customers

About three years before I met Mr. Chan, he opened a gourmet Chinese restaurant on a busy street in a nice area of town. His dream restaurant had come true, and he envisioned tables filled with people relishing the fine food. Yet, business had not picked up since the restaurant opened. Seldom was a night the patrons' conversations reached that pleasant hum of a crowd he longed to hear.

Mr. Chan hired me for a Feng Shui reading, and he met me in the parking lot as I pulled up. As we both stepped through the restaurant doorway, I was stopped in my tracks by the presence of a huge ornamental Chinese screen that stood directly in front of me. It was very detailed, with a black background color. But the dimly lit entryway, combined with the screen, blocked any light that shone from inside the restaurant. I had a claustrophobic sensation, as if I had to squeeze by to enter the dining area.

I shared with my anxious client that the dark, poorly lit entrance was made to seem even more dark and narrow by the huge screen. He explained that it was a very beautiful piece and wanted to display it at the entry. He also thought it would serve to provide the diners privacy from outside foot traffic. However good his intentions, the effect it created made potential patrons feel uneasy, and hesitant to enter. Because the screen was so large and close to the door, it essentially pushed everyone away: it deflected good incoming Qi (and customers!). The screen seemed gloomy. Often darkness suggests uncleanliness. You can't be sure

172

how clean a place is when it is hidden in darkness.

I recommended that three or four tables near the entrance be removed, allowing room to place the screen a few feet further back. I told him to install more lighting in this larger entry, and to train two spotlights on the screen. This would accentuate the screen's bright reds, blues, and light jade colors.

To help bring in patrons, I suggested placing a large aquarium in the center of the restaurant, lit to show off some bright tropical fish.

A few weeks after Mr. Chan made the improvements, my wife, children, and I went there for dinner. He greeted us warmly, saying business had picked up substantially. My wife remarked that the food was delicious, and we enjoyed ourselves immensely.

Summary

A large percentage of restaurants fail within the first three years of opening. Since atmosphere is at least 60 percent of what attracts diners, could undesirable Feng Shui be a major factor in those cases? A combination of service, food quality, location, and atmosphere makes for a successful restaurant. Of course this is true, but the impression left on the unconscious from the comfort level and pleasant ambience stays with us long after the meal is over. Could that be why people will choose one breakfast spot over another, even though it has lousy coffee?

Quarreling Over Sharp Corners

A while back, a woman suffering from headaches came to me for acupuncture. According to traditional Chinese medical diagnosis, her headaches mostly stemmed from emotional causes. The basic premise of Chinese Medicine is to heal the whole person, which may also include evaluating the living environment. As I became acquainted with her through the course of treatment, it became apparent that bad Feng Shui was the likely cause of her emotional stress.

She told me that she and her husband of ten years were quarreling more frequently. They were constantly aggravating one another, and the smallest incident would set them off. She was quite concerned—in the past they had gotten along well and enjoyed each other's company immensely.

I asked her what she thought was causing these problems. She had gone over it many times in her own mind, and really did not know. Their lives were pretty good by most standards. Both enjoyed their careers, and they were financially stable. In fact, she added, they had purchased a lovely new home about six months ago; they should be happy.

After briefly explaining how Feng Shui could help her, I asked her to bring me a sketch of their home's interior. At her next appointment, she brought in the floor plan, which we examined together (see illustration). The entrance from the garage opened into the family room, where they spent most of their time. I told her because of the basic layout, they should have great family harmony.

She gave me a quizzical glance. I smiled, then pointed

out two prominent sharp corners created by the architectural design. One was aimed directly toward the main entryway and the other toward the garage entry.

As with many houses in the United States, they entered through the garage, where their cars were parked. Every time one of them came in either the garage or front door entrances, they were met by a view of a sharp corner. Eventually, the impression from the obtrusive corners became imprinted on their minds, and began to cause sharp—or you could say argumentative—emotions to arise.

I gave her a couple of possibilities to correct the Feng Shui. I suggested that the sharp corners be redesigned into more gentle, curved lines. Or place something decorative to

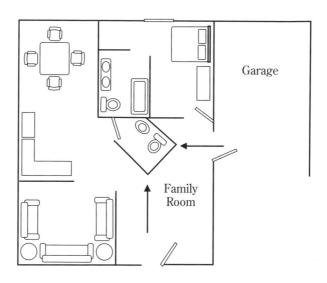

The corners, as shown by the arrows, are aimed directly toward both the garage door entrance and the main entrance of the house. Over a period of time the energy from this "secret arrow of Qi" can adversely affect the subconscious mind.

175

cover the corners, like large plants. This tidbit of Feng Shui made sense to her, and it was inexpensive. She loved plants and rushed to the garden shop.

At her next appointment she excitedly told me things were improved between her and her husband since she put plants in front of both sharp corners. The third week she mentioned they were far more patient and amiable toward one another. They did argue occasionally, but much less frequently than before. She laughed, because she didn't tell her husband why she bought the plants. He was the skeptical sort, and had no idea what was going on. I jokingly said I hoped she didn't use cactus plants, because it would make the corners even sharper! Anyway, I added, it didn't matter if he believed in Feng Shui, it still worked.

Summary

It is a rule of thumb to avoid a view of a sharp object pointing directly toward you. Sharp corners create "secret arrows or knives of Qi." This kind of Qi is aggresive in nature and can cause feelings of agitation and restlessness. If you can't remove or alter the pointed object, you can obstruct your view of it, or hide it with a pleasant object.

You can also hang a mirror opposite the corner to reflect the sharp corner Qi. A decorative mirror can be used which fits your particular taste. In addition, there are specially designed convex Feng Shui mirrors that not only reflect but minimize negative Qi.

Doors to Lasting Love

Janell had a long list of doctors she had seen for her digestive disturbances. Because of her frequent bouts of diarrhea, she always had to be sure a bathroom was readily available.

Janell became increasingly fatigued and depressed, and her personal and professional demands became too much to handle. Within a six-week period, her emotional state further deteriorated, as did her health and patience. Her performance at work suffered, and a substitute was hired to replace her. The relationship with her husband Tom was becoming strained. Finally, he phoned me upon recommendation of a friend who knew me.

In his voice I perceived desperation. Everything else they tried had not helped Janell very much. After we talked for a few minutes, he decided to schedule a Feng Shui reading.

When Tom opened the front door, I could see clear through the house to the backyard. Beginning with the front door, three doors stood in a straight line with one another. Three or more doors in a straight line not only makes for a drafty hall, but is bad Feng Shui. The Qi accelerates down the unobstructed hall and then zooms out the back door, leaving an energetic void. This Qi depletion may manifest in the residents as health problems, especially involving digestion, and personal conflicts may arise.

I advised them to keep the middle door closed, or to place a screen in the pathway to slow the harsh Qi flow. They could also hang a crystal or a wind chime in the hall near the middle door. The idea behind these suggestions was to contain some of the Qi inside the house. Within two weeks of placing a screen in the path of the aligned doors, they began to see remarkable improvements in Janell's health and demeanor. As she grew stronger, she and Tom argued less frequently, and once again they had a happy, healthy relationship.

There is a similar story about two attorneys who shared a law practice in Hong Kong. Disagreements between them had grown to where their business had become dysfunctional, and they were losing money. They commissioned a Feng Shui master, who upon entering their office immediately felt their business was at stake. As in the first story, three doors were aligned, and the vital Qi completely escaped through a double glass door in the back. They were advised to place a barrier in the pathway. The two lawyers hung a large plant near the back door to serve that purpose.

Summary

A home is meant to be a place of nourishment where you receive comfort, food, sleep, and rejuvenation—it is meant to be a Qi reservoir. When three doors, or sometimes two doors, are aligned creating a straight line, it creates what is appropriately termed in Chinese as "straight arrow Qi." Straight lines accelerate the Qi flow, making it harsh and destructive.

However, a house is not meant to be bottled up. There should be a natural flow and presence of vital Qi, fresh air, and natural light. Windows, if not too large, will do this without causing a state of depletion. Just think of Qi as a fresh breeze or a welcome guest. Qi should move serenely, gently touching and inspiring everyone and everything.

Broker's Hungry Kitchen

One of my acupuncture patients owned a "Letter of Credit Brokerage" business. I was treating him for gastrointestinal problems, of which he had a long history. He was somewhat overweight, and asked for help to control his appetite. He also wanted to be treated for stress due in part to the frustration he felt in his work. It seemed he invested a lot of time and energy with substantially less return. There was considerable improvement in his health using acupuncture and herbal therapy, but he never fully recovered. He would return after a period of time for treatments when his ailments recurred.

When a close friend told me that he was interested in starting an international trading business, I immediately thought of this particular patient because of his brokerage experience. I called him to set up a business dinner for the three of us, and we met at a restaurant the following week. Afterwards, the brokerage owner was kind enough to invite us to his home for coffee, and to wrap up the meeting.

I suspected his chronic recurring health problems might be due in part to his living environment; therefore, I took the opportunity to check the Feng Shui of his home. My suspicions were confirmed when I found that his master bedroom door directly faced the kitchen door. This arrangement is not ideal, especially since these two rooms have very different purposes. It created a condition of conflicting energies. But the real imbalance was that the kitchen door was noticeably larger than the bedroom door.

The satisfying dinner and a couple of drinks made us feel very sociable and relaxed. It was an opportune time to talk about Feng Shui. I explained that the dominating energy from the larger kitchen door will, over a period of time, cause health problems related to digestion. I said that this particular door situation may also cause one to feel restless and unproductive. One might leave projects incompleted, and feel unable to accomplish anything.

I suggested a temporary solution: put mirrors lengthwise on the left and right sides of the bedroom door. This would create the illusion that the bedroom door was wider than the kitchen door. The mirrors would also serve to reflect away the Qi from the kitchen. I also told him a permanent solution would be to enlarge the bedroom door, or reduce the size of the kitchen door. Another possible solution would be to move either one of the doors out of alignment with the other and, therefore, away from the other's energetic influence.

Summary

It is bad Feng Shui when a larger kitchen door faces a smaller bedroom door, because the kitchen becomes the dominant force and wants to "swallow up" the bedroom door. Such an influence may cause the occupants to be consumed with thoughts of food, or with the desire to dine out often. If someone is overweight, despite efforts to lose weight, or has other health problems related to digestion, it may be a sign to check their door proximities and sizes.

Facing doors are not necessarily bad Feng Shui, but there are some "facing door size" situations that can have negative influences. For example, if a larger bathroom door faces a smaller bedroom door, the person will most likely have bladder problems. They will also be compelled to go out, instead of relaxing at home. If a larger closet or storage door faces a smaller bedroom door, the person may become stressed by feeling out of control, unorganized, and messy.

Contractor's Cool Pool

Gerry was a licensed contractor who had good business sense, and always had work, even in slow times. Since he started his own business eight years ago it had steadily grown, and was doing quite well. When I met him, he had just finished the last improvements on his home. A mutual friend brought me to a barbecue Gerry had at his house to celebrate the completed project.

We walked into Gerry's house through to the backyard barbecue. I habitually noticed the Feng Shui on the way through the house, and made a mental note of a hallway with two bathroom doors facing each other.

The party was casual and relaxed, and Gerry was a gregarious host. Eventually, we struck up a conversation, and I told him about acupuncture and Feng Shui. As we continued talking, Gerry confided that although his business was successful, he never seemed to have a sizable return in profit for all the work and growth that had occurred the last two years. He waved his hand over the large backyard, and sighed that he didn't even have enough money for a pool. He had originally budgeted for it two years ago when he started the project because he enjoyed pool parties, but now had to wait.

This was a perfect time to explain what he could do to improve his financial situation. I explained that two facing bathroom doors were like two negative poles at odds with each other. To break the conflicting energy, he could hang a crystal or a wind chime between the two doors. Gerry was fascinated by this idea. He decided to hang the chimes.

Besides, they would make pleasant sounds in the hallway cross breeze.

When I received a call from Gerry five months later, I had forgotten about the conversation we had, so it took me a minute to remember what we spoke about. He said there was more profit from his business, and that he had finally built an elegant pool. Gerry invited me and my family over for dinner to thank me. When we arrived, Gerry handed me a Hung Bao (traditional Chinese cash gift given in a red envelope) to show his appreciation. He certainly impressed me as a first-rate host, as he took the effort to make payment for a Feng Shui reading in the traditional Chinese way.

Summary

Facing doors are not always bad Feng Shui, the exception being two bathroom doors. A bathroom is a place where unclean, negative energy is eliminated, so a bathroom door is a negative force. Two bathroom doors create a situation of opposing negative forces. This may cause problems with the middle of the body, in other words, digestion and elimination. The situation may also manifest as financial difficulties. You may feel as if money is slipping away uncontrollably. Breaking the energy lock was simple—a distracting wind chime was placed between the two doors.

Facing doors may also cause problems if they are obviously overlapping or askew. The misalignment makes an uneven view. The "off-centeredness" of the doors may eventually lead to a misunderstanding between their residents. A mirror can be placed on the overlapping wall to help bring visual balance.

Well-Behaved Windows

Some good friends invited my wife and me to a summer dinner party. We had not seen them for quite some time, and were excited about getting together.

During our visit, I noticed that the high ceilings, large windows, and large rooms made the house feel open and airy. Before dinner, I stood with my host in their dining room, near a huge window which had an exquisite view of the bay. Suddenly, there was a commotion in the kitchen, where our hostess Jean was reprimanding her two little boys. Her voice was calm, but as the children's voices escalated, she shut the door, put them to bed and returned to her guests.

She was obviously embarrassed and apologized for the incident. We all assured her there was no need to apologize; everyone there had children and dealt with such things before. As dinner began, this led us into a discussion about our children. Jean was concerned because the boys were becoming increasingly more argumentative and uncooperative. They were also misbehaving in school.

Before leaving that night, I took Jean aside to talk about the Feng Shui of their house, and what could be done to improve the relationship with their boys. I told her that a house we had a couple of years ago also had many large windows, some much larger than the doors. After a period of time I realized that this imbalance was creating problems with the children—they started talking back to us.

My solution was to string bells around the doorknobs, which jangled whenever the doors were used. This strange yet simple solution proved to be effective: my children were nicer to be around. We were able to resolve difficulties with calm discussion and gentle discipline.

Two weeks later, I phoned Jean and her husband to thank them for the evening. She took the unusual advice I gave her, and had hung bells on the doorknobs the next day. She noticed the boys were minding her better. They seemed much more reasonable, instead of constantly arguing. They even surprised her by improving in school.

Summary

In Feng Shui, the doors represent the position of parents. They serve more functions, and have more control over the distribution of Qi in a house than windows do. Because the doors represent the mouth (commands) of the parents, they should have more influence than the windows do, which represent the mouth (response) of children. If the windows are larger than the doors, the children are in a position of dominance over their parents' authority. Hanging bells, or any pleasant "noise maker" on the doorknob, puts the door in a position of dominance over the windows: the windows must "listen" to the doors when they make a sound or "speak."

There are many solutions to the door and window size problem. Larger windows could be visually reduced by adding curtains and valance. A door could have mirroring or framing added to the sides to make it appear larger.

Windows should not be shorter than average height, or too narrow or slit-like. The constraint in Qi flow will possibly cause missed opportunities, or may promote an attitude of having a "narrow perspective" on life.

Pizza Shop's Low Overhead

While attending a seminar on the Northwest coast, I was approached by one of the other participants, who heard I gave Feng Shui readings. He was concerned about his brother's pizza shop in a small coastal town. Neither of them could understand why the restaurant was doing so poorly. His brother had chosen the location carefully, and was as thorough with design and decor as he was with the quality of food. He asked if I would give a reading for his brother's shop; he would show me some of the beautiful countryside on the drive. I took him up on his offer, since it coincided with my plans to relax for a couple of days while I was there.

The little town was charming, and the pizza shop was in a great location, as he told me earlier. My new friend introduced me to his brother. At first glance, I was immediately aware of the Feng Shui problem—the ceiling was too low.

The restaurant was on the first floor of a two-story building, so the ceiling could not be reconstructed to be any higher than it was. Regardless of this limitation, I assured him that we could dramatically improve the Feng Shui using a little creativity. I gave specific instructions, and they listened intently. I suggested that the entire back wall be mirrored. The ceiling should be painted black, and the light fixtures should be replaced with ones that would not reflect light off the ceiling; specifically, track lighting or canister lights that supplied light in a downward direction only.

The resulting effect from these changes made the ceiling appear higher. It was difficult to tell its actual height. The dark color created the illusion that it was higher, and the lighting was specifically chosen to give it even more depth. Mirroring the back wall visually enlarged the dining area. This combination was very effective to open and expand the space. It also created a classy, sophisticated look.

Summary

Even in a large room a low ceiling may feel claustrophobic. The pizza shop's ceiling was an extreme case—it seemed low enough to bump your head. Ceiling height is an important consideration in places of business, since the objective is to draw customers inside.

Generally, ceilings should be high, light in color, and have plenty of lighting. It is usually not desirable to use black extensively in decorating. But in this case, the qualities of black, emptiness and darkness, were instrumental in making a ceiling that was too low appear less noticeable, and actually higher than it was.

Black does not necessarily convey undesirable qualities; it is merely an opposite, existing in mutual Yin/Yang relationship with white. However, black does express grief, emptiness, and darkness, and it may lead to feelings of uncertainty. Black is also associated with the making of money, contemplation, and the quality of depth.

The Suspicious Gourmet

One morning, Chris called my office wondering if I had a moment to talk. She was an artistic and sensitive person prone to feelings of nervousness. But lately she was overwhelmed and controlled by it. She was also becoming short-tempered with her husband. These emotions were usually the worst around the time she was preparing dinner, and when he came home from work. She was concerned because this pattern was beginning to affect the couple's personal relationship.

Chris was a wonderful cook; in her youth she had taken lessons at a well-known culinary school. She found cooking to be a great creative release. The food she prepared was not only delicious, but beautifully presented. Recently though, she was less happy about being in the kitchen.

She asked how much I charged for a Feng Shui reading because she was on a fixed budget. I told her I thought I could do a reading over the phone, if she could clearly explain everything, and if the problem was uncomplicated.

From what she told me so far, I thought the kitchen was the best place to start. I asked Chris to visualize facing the stove, cooking. Then I asked her to explain the layout of the house from where she was.

"Well," she began, "the stove faces east toward a wall which divides the kitchen from the dining room. Behind me is a long hallway that leads to the bedroom, living room, and bathroom."

I realized that Chris was cooking with her back to a

major entryway. I asked her to describe her feelings. She had the peculiar sensation of being "snuck up on," causing her to be fearful and jumpy. She was easily startled by her husband when he came home from work.

When she stood at the stove, she was in a vulnerable position. She was unable to see what was going on around her, or who was in the house. I told her as a master chef she should also be master of her environment—in command of what was around her.

For a convenient solution, I suggested she hang a mirror above the stove, so she could see everything around her. This would dispel her fearful and suspicious feelings. At first, Chris was skeptical that this simple solution would relieve her seemingly complex emotional state. I told her she wouldn't lose anything if she tried it. Two weeks later, she called with some good news. She was feeling much calmer and happier. She also had baked a tray of holiday goodies for my family.

Summary

Spending time anywhere, especially in the kitchen, with your back toward a major entryway is not good Feng Shui. This was crucial in Chris's case, because the front door was in direct view from the kitchen. She could not feel relaxed or concentrate on what she was doing, because she was subconsciously compelled to "keep an eye" on the front door.

Actually, it is best to be in a position where you can see what is happening all around you—in the position of command. This applies to a work space, office, kitchen, or bedroom.

In Feng Shui the kitchen represents "wealth" or "finances"—quality food means prosperity. The cook should have a pleasing, well-lit, open area where he or she is in complete control.

The kitchen is the "stomach and intestines" of the home. It has traditionally been a gathering place, because food is an expression of love. It is important to have a happy cook because the heart is transmitted into everything that is served. If the kitchen has a negative atmosphere, the food may absorb unhappy elements.

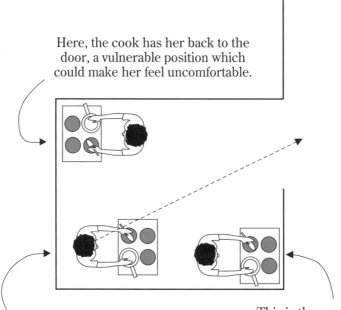

Here, the cook has her back to the door, a vulnerable position which could make her feel uncomfortable.

The best choice for the cook is here. She can see what is happening all around her, and has control of her environment.

This is the second best choice for cook to stand because she can see the doorway.

Student's Rearranged Room

Veronica was a young college student who always enjoyed school, and was taking a full load that semester. However, in the last six months, she started having severe migraines and insomnia. On nights she suffered from insomnia, the migraines would be worse, and then her terrible migraines would cause her to lose sleep. Thus, a vicious cycle was perpetuated, and it was affecting her studies.

After a course of acupuncture treatments, her condition vastly improved. Each time I thought the case was near resolution, I started to schedule her treatments further apart. But after a short while, her migraines and insomnia would return as before. When her migraines returned for the third time, I reexamined her case according to the parameters of traditional Chinese Medicine, and found nothing significant that created her persistent problems. It was possible that Veronica was adversely affected by her living environment, and I decided to talk to her about it at her next appointment.

When Veronica walked into my office, I greeted her, handed her a piece of paper and a pencil, and asked her to sketch a layout of her apartment, including furniture, doors, windows, and so on. She was momentarily surprised, and was going to ask me why, but stopped and began sketching because I had already left to remove another patient's needles. When I returned and motioned her to the next available treatment room, I explained my strange request, and we started to discuss her drawing.

Veronica shared a house with two other students, so she

sketched her room, the hallway and the doors that were close to hers. She said her roommates didn't give her headaches, in fact they got along great. Her bed was immediately in front of the doorway, with the foot of the bed closest to the door. I asked her to sketch the objects in the room immediately opposite hers as well. She quickly sketched and handed me the paper. I laughed, and gently asked, "Did you notice that you are receiving energy from a toilet?" I explained that the furniture in her room was not arranged in the best configuration—it was causing her to feel emotionally uptight. Veronica's eyes misted as she blurted out that she had felt extremely anxious and depressed, and unable to understand why. I suggested she rearrange the furniture in her room, and made a sketch for her on the reverse side of the paper.

Six days later Veronica came for a treatment, and reported her headaches were less frequent, and her sleep was much better. Two weeks later she had further improvement. After four weeks, her symptoms had all but disappeared.

Summary

I did not tell Veronica the furniture arrangement in her room created extremely bad Feng Shui (see illustration). Not only was her bed directly in line with the door, the foot of the bed faced the door. In this vulnerable position you can't see who is entering. Also, the lower body is more vulnerable when your feet face the door. Her door was aligned with the bathroom door, which was usually swung open when not in use. This gave Veronica a first-hand view of the toilet. Even if her door was closed, she subconsciously knew what was behind the bathroom door. So Veronica faced each day facing a toilet! No wonder she had headaches! A bath-room is a place of "Yin" negative energy. We go there to wash away uncleanliness, and it is a place of elimination.

Attention to furniture arrangement is vital to create the best atmosphere and Qi flow, even more so in a small room with only a few objects. The bed should be placed so that there is a comfortable view of the door without being in direct alignment with the Qi flow. This provides a sense of security because the door is in view, yet places the sleeper in a less active, more restful place.

Doesn't it make sense if you were confronted by a less than desirable view every day that over a period of time it would affect you in a negative way?

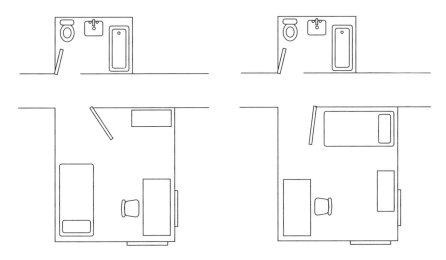

Before (left), the foot of the student's bed faced the doorway that opened directly across from the bathroom, with a view of the toilet. Although this room placement and arrangement (right) is not ideal, the student was no longer affected by the adverse bathroom Qi when she woke in the morning.

Architect's Grand Plan

Freddie was a self-employed architect, working out of his home. His wife was my patient, and I became acquainted with Freddie's business situation during the course of her treatment. Two years ago, Freddie had left the architectural company he was employed with for several years to start his own business. He encountered the usual struggles of a new business owner, but had particular difficulty in managing his employees. It seemed they misinterpreted his instructions, missed important deadlines, or failed to meet his standards for quality. Even though Freddie employed only three people, he was in a managerial crisis, and felt he had little control over his own business. When Freddie worked for a company he was a field foreman, and enjoyed managing the projects and people. Lately, however, he was becoming increasingly depressed and worried over this unexpected problem.

When Jan and Freddie invited me to their home for their ten-year anniversary party, I told them I would be happy to check the Feng Shui for them. From the conversations Jan and I had about Freddie's business struggles, I suspected that bad Feng Shui could be partially responsible.

Freddie gave me a grand tour of their home. He proudly explained improvements he made to it since they purchased it four years ago. The office was of special interest to me, and I asked who sat at each desk. At that point, it became obvious that the room layout was a problem, especially for the boss!

I suggested a furniture rearrangement that would serve to give him "the position of command" in the room. Also, I had

Freddie position his desk so that his back would not face the entry. The person in charge should be able to easily see who enters the room, and be aware of everything going on around him. That is why the corner furthest from the door is the "command position" in a room.

Summary

Actually, the place and position of the boss's desk in the "before" illustration is the worst possible place for it to be. The position or corner closest to the door is the "servant's" position, or in modern context, where the receptionist might sit. Someone entering the office would naturally approach the desk closest to the door to ask a question. The command position of any room is the furthest corner from the main door, where the person in charge should be situated. Also, the boss's desk should not be placed with his back to the door. This arrangement naturally puts you in a vulnerable state. It is difficult to see who is coming and going, and everything is "going on behind your back." Over time, you may find yourself stressed more than usual, or feeling out of control. Neither should the boss have his back to his employees. The best position for the boss is where he can clearly "keep an eye" on them and where they can visually appreciate his presence. Then they are naturally compelled to perform their assigned duties.

This desk-placing rule can be applied to nonbusiness situations as well, such as a private study, den, or a student's study area.

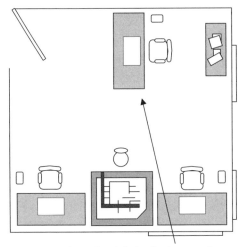

Before, when Freddie's desk was close
to the door, he felt he had little control
over his business and his employees.

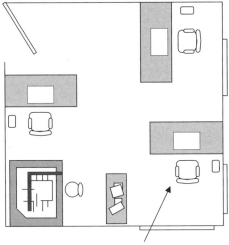

After, Freddie's desk was moved to the far corner
of the office, and he felt more control. His employees
also seemed more responsive and helpful.

Dilemma of the Desks

This story was related to me by one of my students, who recognized that his trouble at work was caused by a case of bad Feng Shui. Names, of course, are fictitious.

When Tim and Susan began working together in a downtown accounting firm, they hit it off right away. In fact, Tim was initially attracted to Susan she was gregarious, yet sensitive and considerate. Their first week on the job together Tim noticed how friendly and helpful she was, more so than his own reserved nature. But as time passed, the relationship became strained and uncomfortable. In three months' time she had constructed an invisible wall around herself. Tim could not understand why she withdrew from him, even after he carefully asked if there was anything he had done to upset her. It became difficult for them to work together because of the communication breakdown, and antagonistic undertones. The more he extended himself, the further she retreated.

Six months later, Tim and Susan received the same promotion they had both applied for, and were moved to another office that they would again share. It was similar to their previous office, except that their desks were arranged differently. Tim soon noticed a change in Susan's attitude toward him. She seemed more relaxed and opened up again, becoming as friendly and warm as before. Eventually, they started taking their lunch break together, and became steadfast friends.

Summary

In their first office, Susan and Tim's desks were directly facing each other. Susan felt she had no privacy, no means of escape. She was confronted head-on by Tim's presence, and the fact that he was attracted to her magnified the tense atmosphere.

Two desks directly facing each other create a state of "opposing forces." This opposing Qi is like that of two rams butting heads and locking horns. The situation of directly opposed Qi creates a high-pressure environment, which can lead to emotional tension and an argumentative energy. The desks in the new office were placed more at right angles so that they were not directly facing each other. Once Susan was in this more comfortable work space, she was able to relax and let down her guard. The simple rearrangement provided a better working environment.

Imagine how businesses could improve employee production and morale just by proper placement of their work stations or desks. If two desks directly face each other, even placing them slightly askew will break the energetic lock. Also, a large plant or similar object can be placed between two opposing desks to ease tensions.

Place in the Company

One of my friends in Los Angeles, Mr. Liu, owned an import/export company that dealt with medical equipment such as surgical gloves, scissors, and other small supplies. He worked mainly with Asian countries, and had numerous contacts. When he first started his business, he was very industrious, invariably working 14-hour days. He always seemed to have a phone glued to his ear, and wore his beeper the rest of the time. For two years he operated at this level of intensity, and then evaluated his financial progress. He discovered there wasn't an equitable profit margin in relation to the growth of sales. More than once, he had struggled to make payroll for his five employees.

Finally, he asked me to do a Feng Shui reading for his business and home. We went first to his place of business. The reception/customer lounge was simply decorated and had good Feng Shui. Mr. Liu's office, though small, was not in a bad location or arranged poorly. The employee office was much larger, and the desks were acceptably arranged. I told him the general layout was actually very good. Mr. Liu juggled his ever-present cell phone, and proudly stated that he studied a Feng Shui book to design his offices. I nodded, but I wanted to further investigate the employees' office. I asked who sat at each desk and their job assignment. Mr. Liu introduced me to each person and explained their duties. He added that they were all excellent employees.

After the introductions, I understood why Mr. Liu was struggling with his finances and expansion. The desks were not positioned poorly; the problem lay in the seating arrangement. He had placed his bookkeeper's and financial manager's desks closest to the door. The other three employees' desks were behind, their work encompassing sales. I suggested that Mr. Liu have the bookkeeper move his desk in the corner of the room furthest from the door, and the financial manager move her desk directly in front of the bookkeeper's (see illustration). Then the three salespersons' desks should be moved closest to the door.

Six months later, Mr. Liu came to my house, bringing food and Mao Tai (a quality Chinese liquor) to show his gratitude for the Feng Shui reading. His business had turned around. He picked up some new contracts, and was now showing a comfortable profit. I noticed he was very relaxed. He also wasn't wearing his beeper or carrying a cell phone.

Summary

When setting up an office, it is important that the employees' desks are arranged according to their duties. For example, the bookkeeper and financial manager handle company money. It is not good to have them nearest to the door. Traditionally, the handling of money is done in a more private place, not out in the open—your profits should be protected. It is much better to have the money handlers in the rear of the room with other desks in front to serve as a protective barrier.

Also, the salespeople should be seated closest to the door to bring in business. It is the most appropriate place for them to "reach out and bring in sales."

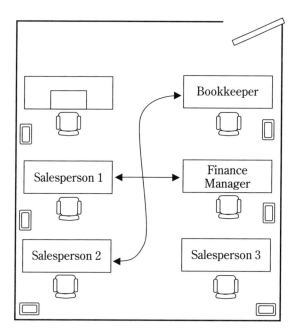

Before, the bookkeeper and finance manager sat in the positions shown, near the door. A simple switch with the two salespersons' desks improved the energetics for a business situation, as explained in the story.

Oversupplemented Warehouse

A healthcare professional asked me to do a Feng Shui reading for him. He also was a major distributor for vitamins and other supplements. When asked what prompted him to call me, the doctor paused a moment, then told me he actually had quite a busy practice. His problem seemed to be in controlling the cash flow. He spent a lot of money, but couldn't keep track of where it was going. It was confusing to discern which expenses were necessary and which were not. He sighed and explained he felt like he was pushing a huge boulder uphill: he was working much harder than he anticipated, and felt out of control of his business.

We met at his office, which was located in an affluent part of town. The office layout and location did not have any particular Feng Shui errors. However, when he ushered me into the warehouse where his nutrients were stocked, my eyes had to adjust to the dim light. I could barely make out the rows of narrow shelves which filled the room. When I asked how much stock was on hand, he shrugged. He wasn't sure if there was enough for the upcoming week.

Back at his office, I suggested running a printout of the inventory. We sat and analyzed the sheets together, and I pointed out that, in fact, he was greatly overstocked on about half of the nutrients. The inventory could be reduced by 50 percent or more, which would generate better cash flow. I then suggested a few things to improve the Feng Shui in the warehouse. He should definitely increase the lighting to see more clearly. I also suggested opening up the area by rearranging the shelves so they weren't stacked so closely together. The deep, narrow shelves should be replaced with wider, shallower ones that would display supplies so they could be seen at a glance.

It was also necessary to update his software capabilties to do real-time inventory control. That way he could save time and be more organized.

Summary

Even with a clear and logical list, the darkness and clutter in the warehouse caused the doctor to have feelings of insecurity and confusion. A primary rule of Feng Shui is to keep your environment clean and organized. If a Feng Shui master came to your home, and you fixed everything he told you, but your house was dirty, cluttered, and disorganized, then you will still have an unhealthy environment. The Feng Shui corrections would be nullified. "Cleanliness is next to godliness," and it is also good Feng Shui.

Declining Cash Register

A young man attended one of my Feng Shui seminars, where he realized that his father's business difficulties were not necessarily caused by mismanagement or bad luck. He eventually talked his father into getting a Feng Shui reading from me.

The 50-year-old owner decided about a year ago to open a convenience store in the downtown area. He was paying higher rent than he had budgeted for, but the store was in an excellent location, with plenty of foot traffic. Although everything about the store seemed to predict financial success, business was rather slow. As time passed, he was actually struggling to make a living.

As we stood talking in the doorway of his store, I took in the layout at a glance, seeing immediately where he could correct the Feng Shui. The owner had placed the cash register directly under an inclined wall that slanted at about 35°. The wall was actually the underside of a stairway directly on the other side. This illusion made the wall appear as if it were going downward into a void. I suggested moving the cash register nearer to the front window and placing a large, healthy plant in front of this angled space. The plant would bring new life to the area, and detract attention away from an energetic dead zone. I asked the store owner to call me in a few weeks to let me know how business was going.

About four weeks later he called as I was leaving my office for lunch. He said at first he thought it was his imagination, but his receipts showed that business had indeed picked up—

and was getting busier with each passing week. He also thanked me for the advice. I told him to first thank his son for his thoughtful suggestion to try Feng Shui. The man laughed and said I just gave him the idea to offer his son a share of the business. I said it would be a good move, since his son obviously had a keen sense for business.

Summary

In Feng Shui, the best structures are designed with balance and symmetry. This imparts a stable, balanced energy to a room or dwelling. It is not ideal to build a structure that has slanted walls, sharp corners, or steeply sloped ceilings. Sharp, acute angles create energetic dead zones and Qi tends to pool in these areas. Practically speaking, these corners are not very usable, suitable only for things you want to "throw in the corner." A slanted wall can create feelings of instability; the mind tends to believe what it sees—an unstable-looking wall. A slanted wall that leads the eye downward, draws Qi downward as well.

A sloped or vaulted ceiling is less preferable in Feng Shui, because it creates an imbalanced, unstable Qi flow. To help correct the Feng Shui, hang lights from the high end of a sloped ceiling that extend to the level of the low end. This visually brings everything to one level—and it is an elegant addition that will not compromise the design.

Red Cloth Overkill

A very sophisticated woman came into my clinic one Monday. I ushered her into a treatment room and began going over her case. As it turned out, she had carpal tunnel syndrome. Her tennis game had suffered considerably because of it, and she wanted an alternative to surgery. She also asked about treatment for stress. The financial problems from a small specialty clothing store she owned were taking their toll on her.

She brought up the subject of Feng Shui, adding that a friend talked about a class I taught on it. It was of interest to her because she was an interior designer on the side.

As I inserted the acupuncture needles I asked her about the location, size, and layout of the store. The image she created made me realize that a fresher color was needed on the walls than the brownish-beige she described. I also told her to place a bright red cloth underneath the cash register. I told her that many Chinese restaurants have a red cloth underneath their cash registers to generate cash flow.

At her next treatment she proudly reported she had the walls painted a lighter color, and had placed a candy apple red cloth under the cash register.

During the next four weeks of acupuncture treatment her wrists quickly improved. As she was leaving from her last appointment she asked to speak to me in private. Her stress was somewhat relieved, but not completely. Her finances were still a major burden. She then politely informed me the store had counted an even greater loss that month, despite the improved Feng Shui.

After a moment, she apologized, noting my advice was free after all, and she was grateful for my help. I then told her that I would like to stop by the store for a consultation. She was so happy that she almost lost her cool composure, but quickly recovered, and said that I could choose a beautiful scarf for my wife as a gift for going out of my way.

Her specialty clothing store looked quite impressive from the street as I parked my car. I quickly walked in to greet her. The cash register was placed just off to the left in the store, which is a good place for it. But then I saw a large bulky object underneath it. She patiently reminded me that I had instructed her to place a red cloth there. I tried to lift the cash register and she helped pull out the cloth. It was huge. I laughed as I unfolded it. I pulled it back and forth, trying to spread its entire size, which was about eight by twelve feet.

The show was entertaining, and she laughed with me, not really knowing what was so amusing. Then, I gathered up the cloth and said: "This is like a sail, a cloth just a little larger than the cash register is the proper size. Overdoing a Feng Shui cure may nullify the intended effect. It is amazing how people often believe in every situation 'if a little is good, a lot is much better.' " She slowly shook her head in agreement and smiled warmly—then led me to the scarves where I was to choose a gift for my wife.

Summary

A Feng Shui solution may not instantly bring us wealth or position. Everything must be balanced, including the intended cure. If it looks out of place or interferes with regular business, then the enhancement will not work. The red cloth was too large and the cash register teetered upon it. The intended cure made the cash register unstable. The fact that the store suffered even more financial loss after that proves that balance is important in more ways than one!

Open Beam Dream

Robert came to my office complaining of insomnia, headaches, and digestive problems. Otherwise, the 38-year-old architect was in excellent physical condition. After a few acupuncture treatments he was feeling measurably better, but was still troubled by insomnia. He slept soundly in my office, lying on a little treatment table with acupuncture needles in place. Ironically, he tossed and turned all night in his own bed with its comfortable mattress. I suspected it was bad Feng Shui that impaired his sleep at home.

Robert designed the house himself, and it was featured in a recent magazine article. He brought the article with him at my request, so I could check the Feng Shui. The house had a magnificent Southwestern Indian pueblo design. It was rustic and charming, and of course all the ceilings were open-beamed. I immediately turned to the photo of the bedroom to see if my suspicions were correct. Sure enough, the bedroom was open-beamed like the rest of the house, and there was a 4 x 8 cross beam that aligned directly over the middle of Robert's bed.

An open cross beam directly over where you are sitting or sleeping may create uneasy feelings in the subconscious mind, especially in the bedroom. Sleep is a totally vulnerable state—you need to feel completely safe to rest peacefully. The subconscious is profoundly influenced by images projected by our surroundings. To the subconscious mind, the huge open beam appeared precarious. It braced the entire ceiling, yet appeared loosely secured. Logically, Robert knew the ceiling was safe, yet his subconscious perceived otherwise. This imprinted image seemed to be the cause of Robert's continuing insomnia and nervous tension.

To correct the Feng Shui, all Robert had to do was move the bed so that it wasn't directly under the cross beam. He now experiences restful sleep under the open-beamed ceiling that he enjoys so much.

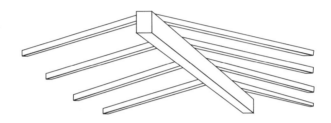

A supporting beam directly over a bed, couch, or any other area where you relax could cause unsettling feelings.

Summary

Southwest-style ceilings with open beams are not necessarily bad Feng Shui. However, one should avoid sleeping or sitting for long periods under either a very large, or a weight-bearing, cross beam.

There are several cures that can waylay uneasiness if the situation cannot be avoided. Two bamboo stalks can be placed on a beam directly above a bed. The stalks should be angled with the root-end lower and the branch-end pointing upward. This creates an upward-moving energy and stability. Also, the beams can be reconstructed as arched to appear more supportive. Or, a false ceiling can be put up.

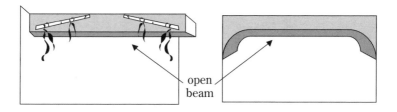

open
beam

Bamboo stalks tied with red ribbons and angled as they
would be growing, (leaf end up) provide uplifting energy.
Or, the cross beam can be constructed as an arch.

The "unstable Qi" perception of someone sleeping under an open beam can be applied to other situations. Obviously, a house under a cliff overhang would feel precarious.

There is an elegant building in a desert preserve nestled among precarious-looking boulders and steep rocky cliffs. The architect intuitively used Feng Shui for a very powerful effect. He built huge, sharply pointed "steeples" on each of the hexagon roofs. These "steeples" counteracted the image of threatening boulders, and energetically protected those inside.

If we are aware, we can see where the Feng Shui is a problem. How does the image projected by a situation impact the subconscious? Does an environment "look and feel" symmetrical, harmonious, and balanced?

Mary's Mirror Mishmash

After she experienced a particularly difficult night of sleeplessness with several anxiety attacks, Mary's husband urged her to get help. She decided to try acupuncture as an alternative to sleeping pills. When Mary came to my office, she was obviously distraught and exhausted.

She confided in me about the strange and frightful experiences she had while trying to sleep. Her husband said she was very restless at night, and would sit up in her sleep and ask who was there. Sometimes she would shout at that "someone" to get out of the room.

This woman, known by her friends for her tenacious and courageous personality, had suddenly become afraid at night, and she couldn't understand why.

About three months ago her strange symptoms started occurring. I also learned they had redecorated their home only four-and-a-half months ago. I immediately thought the redecorating may have created bad Feng Shui. I explained that a holistic plan for treatment, including acupuncture and herbs, would also require a Feng Shui reading for their home.

Mary was a prominent media personality, who also had a flair for interior design. Her home was spacious and elaborate, with an open and airy feeling, and the decor was perfectly accentuated throughout. The master bedroom had two large mirrors placed directly opposite each other to enhance the room size. One mirror was mounted on a closet door that was in front of their king-size bed, and the second mirror hung behind the bed, reflecting the closet mirror.

Judging from Mary's symptoms, the likely cause of her unsettling insomnia was caused by the bedroom mirror placement. Because the two mirrors faced each other, she saw her reflection repeated infinitely whenever she looked at the mirrored closet door. Over a period of time, it was imprinted on her subconscious mind that she was in a room with a great number of people. No wonder she screamed for them to leave while she was dreaming . . . it was getting rather crowded in there!

Within a week after removing the mirror on the door, Mary's anxiety and insomnia were all but resolved. Her husband was spared her experience because a plant at the foot of his side of the bed blocked his reflection. If they had decided to keep the mirror, the next best solution would have been to block Mary's reflection as well.

Summary

Bad Feng Shui is often created with mirrors in modern interior decoration. The mirror configuration in this story is a common decorating mistake. Mirrors are very powerful Feng Shui tools to deflect undesirable Qi, and they must be used wisely. Overdoing mirrors can create major problems, or at least confusion. People have been injured by running into walls that have been mirrored from top to bottom. A shoe store in a local mall had every wall mirrored, and even the pillars within the store were mirrored. The mirrors were confusing, and the salesman couldn't tell how many people were in the store, because the mirrors caught every passerby's reflection! As it turned out, the store had been robbed several times that year, probably due in part to the confusing mirrors. The salesman seemed stressed and suffered from chronic headaches. No wonder!

As an enhancement, two facing mirrors can be used in an entry or doorway to open up the area. Because it is a place where people quickly pass through, the reflected images wouldn't have a negative influence on them. In Feng Shui, facing mirrors placed in an entry are thought to cleanse the Qi of a person passing through.

Writer's Cramped Career

Brandon was a professional writer who was well established, and quite well known in the industry. He enjoyed many lucrative years of doing what he loved and excelled in. However, over the past three years he was having difficulty acquiring new contracts. He had become increasingly upset and depressed, which frustrated him and stressed the relationship with Wendy, his wife.

She was a patient of mine, and mentioned her concern for him during one of her appointments. She must have picked up a flyer at my office about a Feng Shui class I was offering, because she called a few months later to schedule a reading. Because Brandon worked in their home, the most important areas to focus on would be those pertaining to "career" and "reputation." Therefore, I decided to use Ba Gwa theory to enhance those areas. (See Chapter 6: Design and Direction, for reference throughout this story.)

According to the Wen-Wang Ba Gwa, the entrance of a house, or room, is the North Gwa, the symbol representing "career." Often, the living room is located at the entrance of the house, which was the case for this couple. Both husband and wife were busy with their individual careers, and they seldom used their living room. They said it was unofficially reserved for special occasions, but even so they rarely used it for entertaining. The plants there weren't well cared for, and were yellow and dying.

I suggested replacing the plants with fresh ones, and playing classical music in the living room. Not only would the music create a pleasant atmosphere, it might help keep the plants alive. I also suggested an aquarium near the living room door to bring new life and activity.

The reputation is expressed in the South Gwa, so I walked further into the house and focused my attention on that room (the "reputation" area of the entire house). This was located at the family room. The South Gwa position of the room was at the fireplace. It was dirty and neglected. It looked kind of bare and broken down, like a burned out tree stump! Dust and ashes had been left there for a long time, and there was no painting or decoration above the fireplace. What Brandon needed was increased demand for his talents—therefore, it was vital to enhance this area. I suggested he clean it up, and purchase fireplace tools and an ash screen that were a gold color. I proposed a nice painting above the fireplace, one that symbolized success or happiness. I left the subject matter up to them, but said that Chinese like pictures of birds in flight. A sea gull flying high, or a sailboat with bright, full sails, would also be appropriate. I also suggested a spotlight from the ceiling to illuminate the painting. I finally said to be creative and make the fireplace area beautiful and bright.

Brandon was skeptical. He didn't believe "fixing-up" the fireplace would get him a single contract. But his wife was very enthusiastic, and wanted to start making changes immediately. She told me privately that she didn't mind using her own savings to do it.

Three weeks later, Wendy invited me over to their house to see the improvements. She showed me the 40-gallon fish tank, and said she spent $900 on improving the fireplace area. They chose a surrealistic painting with an appropriate theme: cosmic light spreading over the darkness. She wanted to portray the idea that her husband was shedding the light of his talent over the universe. She even hired someone to sweep the chimney. I was pleased with their efforts and told Brandon that from now on his reputation would explode. He shook my hand and thanked me, but I detected a raised eyebrow, revealing his continued skepticism.

Six months later, Brandon came to my clinic to be treated for neck pain. We chatted while I placed the needles. He said everything was going fantastically and that he had almost too many contracts to handle. He was on the computer twelve hours a day. He said the Feng Shui reading caused him to come in for acupuncture—he had too much work! He was completely amazed at his career "explosion" after the reading. He then admitted it must be Feng Shui after all—the series of events were too much of a coincidence.

Summary

The fame area is represented by the Gwa "Fire." The fireplace was in that Gwa position. It was a perfect place for it, a natural enhancement for that location. Since both husband and wife worked from their home, it was even more important for them to enhance this area.

The Ba Gwa was not the only method applied in this Feng Shui reading, but it was the one change that made a dramatic difference for this couple. Choosing the area or areas to enhance is based on the individuals' needs. As always, there must be a harmony and balance attained with any cures that are employed. For example, the traditional tools used for this case were color, light, and the painting. But they did not have incongruous objects everywhere, and the decor and ornaments were not Oriental in flavor. A guest would not recognize the changes as Feng Shui enhancements. Maybe you have been Feng Shui'd in your life and did not even know it! If you ever go to play in Las Vegas, notice the Feng Shui of the exterior and interior of the casinos. It is used quite extensively in their favor, as you might imagine. Unknowing gamblers may have more working against them than just the odds.

Plant Takeover

A young woman, only twenty-two, felt things were not going well for her since she finished college and moved to a small apartment of her own. She often felt irritable and depressed. It finally reached a point where she felt unable to cope on a day-to-day level.

She lived in a colorful beach community where houses nearest to the beach are often congested. But it wasn't that confining in her neighborhood—not enough to create the magnitude of stress my young client had. I knocked on the door, and she answered immediately. I walked in, but had to stop and let my eyes adjust to the dim light. It was early on a sunny afternoon, but it was so dark inside that she had lights on in the two small rooms of her apartment. There were five large windows, but a mass of tangled plants hung at each of them. Plants were on all the windowsills as well. She had quite effectively blocked out the light of day.

Every surface near a light source had a plant. I jokingly asked her, "Do you live in a forest? Are you running a nursery in here?" I asked how many plants she had. She said she had more than thirty large and forty smaller ones. She loved them, and collected different kinds. She even had two windows fashioned with a trellis for climbing vines.

I told her that although she enjoyed them, to reduce the number of plants she had; specifically, cut down to less than half. I also suggested removing the vines on the trellised windows. They could easily thrive with indirect sunlight.

I told her that sunlight and fresh air naturally uplift the

spirit, and to open the windows as much as possible. She didn't open the windows very often because she believed her plants provided enough oxygen.

Three months after the Feng Shui reading, she called to say things had turned around in her life. She loved living in her apartment by the beach, and had resolved some of the issues bothering her. She also didn't feel depressed anymore, and had many projects going to keep her happy.

Summary

Plants are one of the important tools that can improve Feng Shui (see Chapter 7: Tools and Cures). Plants generate a life force, an image of growth and progress. Healthy plants in an environment help people feel alive and active. However, if plants are overgrown or in excess, they will monopolize the life elements in their surroundings. The poor plant lover will starve from energetic malnourishment! This can be compared to a huge tree which saps nourishment from the soil, leaving the perimeter bare. A huge tree's overbearing canopy would block sunlight, and small plants underneath would have difficulty thriving.

In Feng Shui image is everything, and unique plant shapes project different energies. For example, a sharply pointed aloe vera could be placed on the corner of a porch to display its "guardian Qi," or a plant with round leaves resembling coins, such as a jade plant, could be placed near the door of a business, or in the wealth corner to draw in "money Qi." If vine-type plants grow out of control, they can create, and even resemble, tangles of constricting fingers: "grasping or clinging Qi." If vines crawl and entwine over a large surface, this "plant takeover" breeds negative Qi.

But vines can also can bring good Feng Shui. They can be grown to "ground" or connect something to the earth you feel insecure about. Also, in Feng Shui round columns are preferable to square ones. Vines can be trained to cover square columns, to round out their shape and minimize the sharp edges.

Fan Over Bed

Karen was a holistic health practitioner in Southern California. It had been a week since she had slept through the night. Eventually, her exhaustion led her to become nervous and fearful. Karen had thoroughly searched for the cause of her insomnia. She tried various holistic remedies which helped for a while, but the insomnia always returned unresolved. Karen was exasperated—there were no personal issues troubling her, and she was in good health. Even though she had a history of insomnia and nervousness, it had never been this extreme. Karen, who often sought my advice, felt she had exhausted other solutions, and asked me to do a Feng Shui reading.

As I walked through her little house, at first I found nothing out of the ordinary about the Feng Shui that would contribute to Karen's symptoms. She lived alone and decorated her home to be very cozy and personable. The basic layout of the home looked fine, but in the bedroom, I noticed that there was nothing on the wall over the head of her bed. I suggested she hang a large decorative fan there. I explained that the fan is a symbolic weapon of protection. It has a calming effect because it provides comfort. It also has the effect of dispersing and softening the Qi field in a room. I said because she lived alone, she may have often felt vulnerable and a little isolated. She was an independent sort, but did admit she experienced those feelings on occasion.

Two weeks later, Karen was much more composed and rested when she dropped by my office. Without any other form of treatment, she was able to sleep soundly after the fan was hung in her bedroom. A simple solution was found to what might otherwise have been considered a complex situation, involving any number of physical or emotional factors. In this case, a Feng Shui solution was the appropriate, and the only, course of action needed.

Summary

Hanging a fan over the head of the bed is a commonly applied Feng Shui cure. A Native American dream catcher or a restful picture are meaningful adaptations, and can achieve the same effect. Ideally, a bed should have a headboard. It brings a sense of protection and stability to the sleeper.

There are a few other considerations about what is over the head of, or around, your bed. Do not hang something that appears precarious or dangerous near your head. You may be subconsciously affected by that image. A large ceiling fan over any part of the bed may also cause uneasiness. Placing the head of the bed against a wall is preferable to being directly under a large window. A wall is a static, solid object and provides a stable foundation for rest.

Twelve Animals of Harmony

While attending a business meeting in Texas, we dined at a nice Chinese restaurant. I was introduced to the owner, who hired me to do a Feng Shui reading for his place the next day. After the reading, business picked up a little for about two months. However, he still didn't see the increase in profit or clientele he had hoped for. The owner politely complained to me that after he invested money in the Feng Shui adjustments he expected more of a return.

A few months later when I was in town again, he invited me to dinner at the restaurant so we could chat. As an after dinner treat, he opened a bottle of Mao Tai, a quality Chinese liquor. He was an engaging host, and we talked late into the night. We had an open-hearted discussion, and talked about many different things, including his business. He then brought up something he hadn't mentioned before.

There was conflict going on among the personnel. The waiters and waitresses were complaining about each other. The kitchen help were complaining about the waiters and waitresses—even the dishwasher was angry with the second chef. There was mass disharmony in the work place—the employees were very unhappy.

I realized this problem was beyond the Feng Shui solutions I had already given. I told him to have success in business, or anything else for that matter, you must have all three elements of perfection present (see Chapter 3: Three Elements of Perfection). We had already improved the Feng Shui to create the perfect space. We also checked the timing with the I-Ching. And besides, it was the 1980s, a booming time in the economy for service-oriented and restaurant businesses.

But he was missing the element of "perfect people." I told him to investigate the employees' complaints so they could reconcile their differences. I even suggested some of the personnel may need to be replaced. He might also consider managerial changes that would breed less hostility. He had already tried a few different things, such as changing regulations and rearranging employee responsibilities, but the discord inevitably returned.

I said there was yet another possibility using Feng Shui, which could help correct the employees' relationships. He agreed to try it. He was at wits' end with them and hated the thought of letting his experienced help go.

I told him to purchase small toy figurines of each of the twelve animals in classical Chinese astrology: Rat, Ox, Tiger, Rabbit, Dragon, Snake, Horse, Goat, Monkey, Rooster, Dog, and Pig. I instructed him to tie them together with a red string in a chain in the order listed. Then, he should hang the decoration on a wall in the restaurant, one most visible to all the employees—perhaps in the break area or a waiter station.

This decoration would symbolically create the image of harmony between all twelve personalities. Since the personnel were born in different years, the twelve figurines would symbolize every year and personality type. The red string was chosen because it is the color of power, happiness, luck, celebration, and love. The meaning behind these strung animal toys symbolized all people working together harmoniously.

The owner did as I had suggested with the figurines. He also had a meeting with the employees and explained the meaning of the strange toy decoration. At the same time he asked for their suggestions to improve morale.

A year later, the "toy animals" suggestion I made really seemed to have worked. The employees were happier and there was much less hostility. The owner was overjoyed because the restaurant was attracting more patrons, and consequently more profit.

Summary

Because the employees were working against each other and creating a negative environment, positive Qi that would have been generated from good Feng Shui or from having the "perfect timing" was cancelled out. In this story, Feng Shui was used to help bring about an atmosphere of "harmonious people." Human relationships may not always be simple to resolve—the dynamics are often complex. But personality conflicts do not have to be considered hopeless. Using perfect timing and perfect space can help create an amicable atmosphere, even if the people involved aren't perfect. Besides, who can claim to be perfect?

Additional Information

To order *Shower of Jewels:*
Please mail the handy order form on page 229 or FAX: (858) 277-9037.

For Feng Shui consultations or classes:
The authors are available for Feng Shui consultations by appointment. Dr. Tan has lectured extensively on Feng Shui throughout the U.S. and is available to teach classes. Private parties and seminar agents welcome. For additional information, FAX: (858) 277-9037, or Write: Feng Shui Info, 4550 Kearny Villa Rd., Suite 107, San Diego, CA 92123.

Of interest to all:
Understanding the Qi field, movement, and effect on the environment and ourselves is important to good health. Dr. Richard Tan presents special workshops on Qi Initiation and Cultivation (Qi Gong). In the class, Dr. Tan personally activates the Qi healing system in your body, and teaches everything you need to begin a lifelong practice of Qi Cultivation which will enhance your physical, mental, and spiritual health. For additional information, FAX: (858) 277-9037, or write: Qi Initiation, 4550 Kearny Villa Rd., Suite 107, San Diego, CA 92123.

Of interest to Acupuncturists and others in the health care professions:
Dr. Tan and Stephen Rush have co-authored two books on advanced methods of pain treatment with acupuncture. *Twelve and Twelve in Acupuncture* and *Twenty-Four More in Acupuncture* are invaluable for clinical practice using Dr. Tan's dynamic treatment style. For ordering or additional information, FAX: (858) 277-9037, or write Acupuncture Publicationa, 4550 Kearny Villa Rd., Suite 107, San Diego, CA 92123.

Please check our website - Drtanshow.com, for updates concerning lectures, publications, and more!

ORDER FORM:

To order copies of this book, please fill out this order form and mail to: Dr. Richard Tan, OMD, L.Ac., 4550 Kearny Villa Rd., Suite 107, San Diego, CA 92123.

I would like _____ copies of *Shower of Jewels* at $26.00.
(California residents add 7.75% sales tax or $2.01, making the total $28.01)

Plus $4.00 shipping and handling for each book ordered.
(Mexico and Canada $6.00, Overseas $13.00)

Amount enclosed: _____ Payable to Richard Tan Books
Check, money order, VISA or MasterCard

Expiration Date _____

_____
Name

_____
Address

_____
City, State, Zip

_____
Phone (work and home) (reqired if paying by credit card)